PRAGUE TRAVEL GUIDE 2023 AND BEYOND

Your Complete Travel Guide to Unraveling the Enchanting Heart of Central Europe

By: Erik Gustav

Contents

INTRODUCTION

Welcome to Prague, the enchanting heart of Central Europe. Nestled along the banks of the Vltava River, Prague is a city steeped in history, adorned with stunning architecture, and brimming with a vibrant cultural scene. This travel guide will serve as your compass as you embark on a journey to uncover the treasures of this timeless city, providing you with insights into its rich past, lively present, and promising future.

Prague, with its medieval charm and Baroque elegance, has earned its place among the most beautiful cities in the world. As you stroll through its cobbled streets and gaze upon the majestic Prague Castle, you'll find yourself transported back in time. From the iconic Charles Bridge to the Astronomical Clock, every corner of this city narrates a tale of art, politics, and romance.

Beyond its historical allure, Prague is a city that embraces contemporary culture with open arms. Its thriving arts scene, burgeoning culinary delights, and vibrant nightlife make it a city that caters to all tastes and interests. Immerse yourself in the local culture, mingle with friendly locals, and let the city's spirit captivate your soul.

Whether you're a history enthusiast, an architecture lover, or a traveler seeking new adventures, Prague promises to leave an indelible mark on your heart. So, prepare to be mesmerized by the magic of Prague, as you unravel the secrets of this captivating city.

HISTORY

Prague, the capital city of the Czech Republic, is steeped in rich history and has played a significant role in shaping European culture. Here's an overview of the historical highlights of Prague:

Early History

Prague's history dates back to ancient times, with evidence of settlements as far back as the Paleolithic era. The city's strategic location along the Vltava River made it a crucial trade route and a center of commerce in Central Europe.

Medieval Era

Prague Castle, originally founded in the 9th century, became the seat of Bohemian kings and the heart of political power. Charles IV, the Holy Roman Emperor, transformed Prague into a cultural and intellectual center in the 14th century, founding Charles University and commissioning iconic landmarks such as Charles Bridge and St. Vitus Cathedral. The Hussite Wars of the 15th century saw religious conflicts, with Jan Hus's teachings leading to the Hussite movement.

Renaissance and Habsburg Rule

The 16th century brought the flourishing of the Renaissance in Prague, with Italian architects contributing to the city's architectural splendor.

The Habsburgs took control of Prague and the Kingdom of Bohemia in the late 16th century, leading to a period of Baroque architecture and cultural growth.

The Defenestration of Prague and the Thirty Years' War

The Defenestration of Prague in 1618 marked the start of the Thirty Years' War, a devastating conflict that significantly impacted the city and the region. Prague was besieged and occupied by various armies during the war, leading to the decline of its population and prosperity.

Austro-Hungarian Empire and Czech National Revival

In the 19th century, Prague became part of the Austro-Hungarian Empire. The Czech National Revival emerged, focusing on the promotion of Czech language, culture, and identity. The National Theater was inaugurated in 1881 as a symbol of Czech national pride.

Czechoslovakia and 20th Century

After World War I, Prague became the capital of newly formed Czechoslovakia. During World War II, the city was occupied by Nazi Germany. The assassination of Reinhard Heydrich in 1942 led to brutal reprisals, including the Lidice massacre. The Velvet Revolution of 1989 brought an end to Communist rule in Czechoslovakia, leading to the peaceful transition to democracy.

Modern Era

In 1993, Czechoslovakia peacefully split into two independent countries: the Czech Republic and Slovakia. Prague has since become a popular tourist destination, renowned for its well-preserved historical architecture, charming Old Town, and vibrant cultural scene.

Traces of the Past Regime

Prague, like many other cities, bears traces of its past regimes, particularly the periods of Nazi occupation and Communist rule. While some of these traces are visible in the form of historical sites, monuments, and architecture, others are more subtle and can be felt through the city's cultural, social, and political fabric. Here are some notable traces of the past regime in Prague:

Communism Museum (Muzeum komunismu):

This museum provides an in-depth look at the Communist era in Czechoslovakia, showcasing propaganda, artifacts, and personal stories from that time.

Memorial to the Victims of Communism:

Located in the district of Újezd, this poignant memorial commemorates the victims of the Communist regime, featuring a line of bronze statues that gradually disappear, symbolizing the gradual disappearance of freedom.

Museum of Communism:

This museum presents a comprehensive overview of life under Communist rule, including propaganda, everyday objects, and interactive displays.

Former Secret Police Headquarters (StB):

The former headquarters of the Communist secret police, located in Bartolomějská Street, is a haunting reminder of the regime's repressive tactics. It is now part of the Security Services Archive.

Prague Spring Memorial:

Located near the National Museum, this monument commemorates the Prague Spring of 1968, a period of political liberalization that was crushed by the Soviet-led invasion.

Jan Palach Memorial:

Jan Palach, a student who self-immolated in protest against the 1968 invasion, is commemorated by a memorial in Wenceslas Square.

Stalin Monument Pedestal:

In Letná Park, the pedestal that once held a giant statue of Stalin now offers panoramic views of the city and serves as a space for cultural events.

Ghost Stations:

During the Communist era, certain metro stations were closed to prevent people from gathering. While some have been reopened, others remain closed and are known as "ghost stations."

Architecture:

Many buildings and landmarks built during the Communist era can still be seen, often characterized by utilitarian design and socialist-realist architecture.

Cultural Influences:

The legacy of the Communist regime is also evident in the city's cultural scene, literature, films, and art created during that period.

TOURIST PRACTICALITIES

Here are some practical tips and information for tourists visiting Prague:

Basic Information

Currency:

The official currency is the Czech koruna (CZK). ATMs are widely available, and credit cards are generally accepted in most establishments.

Public Transport:

Prague has an efficient public transportation system, including trams, buses, and a metro. You can purchase tickets at kiosks, online, or at ticket machines.

Language:

The official language is Czech. English is widely spoken, especially in tourist areas.

Weather:

Prague has a temperate climate, with warm summers and cold winters. Check the weather forecast before your trip and pack accordingly.

Taxi:

Taxis are available, but it's recommended to use reputable companies or apps to avoid scams.

Walking:

Many of Prague's attractions are within walking distance of each other, especially in the historic city center.

Safety:

Prague is generally safe for tourists, but be cautious of pickpocketing, especially in crowded tourist areas. Keep your belongings secure and be aware of your surroundings.

Cultural Etiquette:

Dress modestly when visiting churches and religious sites.

Greet locals with a polite "Dobrý den" (Good day) or "Dobrý večer" (Good evening).

Tipping:

It's customary to leave a small tip (around 10%) for service staff at restaurants, cafes, and bars.

Electricity:

The standard voltage is 230V, and the standard frequency is 50Hz. The plugs are of the European type with two round pins.

Entry Requirements:

Check the visa requirements for your country before traveling to Prague. Citizens of the EU, the U.S., Canada, Australia, and several other countries do not require a visa for short stays.

Time Zone:

Prague is in the Central European Time Zone (CET), which is UTC+1. During daylight saving time (from the last Sunday in March to the last Sunday in October), it follows Central European Summer Time (CEST), which is UTC+2.

Wi-Fi:

Many hotels, restaurants, cafes, and public places offer free Wi-Fi.

Tourist Information Centers:

There are several tourist information centers throughout the city where you can get maps, brochures, and assistance with travel-related queries.

Emergency Numbers:

In case of emergencies, dial 112 for police, medical assistance, or fire services.

Travel Insurance:

It's advisable to have travel insurance to cover unexpected events, such as medical emergencies or trip cancellations.

Accommodation

Prague offers a variety of accommodation options to suit different preferences and budgets. Here are some recommendations for different types of accommodations:

Luxury Hotels:

- Hotel Augustine (Luxury Collection): A luxurious hotel housed in a former monastery, offering elegant rooms and a spa. Located near Prague Castle.

- Aria Hotel Prague: A boutique hotel with themed rooms dedicated to music legends, featuring a rooftop terrace and a music library.

- Four Seasons Hotel Prague: A renowned luxury hotel with stunning views of the Charles Bridge and Vltava River.

Mid-Range Hotels:

- Hotel Paris Prague: A beautiful Art Nouveau hotel located near the Powder Tower, offering comfortable rooms and a stylish restaurant.

- BoHo Prague Hotel: A modern hotel with chic design and a central location, close to major attractions.

- Hotel Residence Agnes: A cozy hotel with personalized service, located in the heart of the Old Town.

Budget and Boutique Hotels:

- Hotel Golden Key: A charming boutique hotel with a historic ambiance, situated in the Lesser Town.

- Hotel Three Storks: A boutique hotel set in a historic building, featuring contemporary design and a great location.

- Charles Bridge Residence: Affordable and cozy apartments near the Charles Bridge and other key sites.

Hostels:

- Czech Inn Hostel: A stylish and modern hostel with a social atmosphere, located a short tram ride from the city center.
- The MadHouse Prague: A fun and lively hostel known for its events and parties, perfect for young travelers.
- Hostel One Home: A sociable hostel with a homey atmosphere, offering free dinners and walking tours.

Apartment Rentals:

- Airbnb: Many private apartments and homes are available for rent on Airbnb, offering a more local experience.
- Booking.com: The website offers a wide range of apartment rentals, allowing you to choose based on your preferences.

Charming Guesthouses:

- Domus Henrici Boutique Hotel: A small and cozy guesthouse with panoramic views of Prague Castle and the city.
- U Zlatého stromu: A historic guesthouse set in a Baroque building, offering a unique atmosphere.

Recommendation: Hotel U Zlate studny

Hotel U Zlaté studně (At the Golden Well Hotel) is a luxurious boutique hotel located in the picturesque area of Prague, Czech Republic. Situated near Prague Castle and offering stunning views of the city, the hotel is known for its elegance, historic charm, and excellent service. Here's an overview of the Hotel U Zlaté studně:

Location:

The hotel is situated in the historic district of Prague, close to Prague Castle and other major attractions. Its address is U Zlaté studně 4/166, 118 00 Prague 1, Czech Republic.

Accommodation:

The hotel offers a range of luxurious and individually designed rooms and suites, each uniquely decorated with attention to detail. Many of the rooms offer breathtaking views of Prague's skyline, including landmarks like Prague Castle and the Charles Bridge.

Dining:

The hotel features an upscale restaurant known for its gourmet cuisine and panoramic views. Guests can enjoy a fine dining experience while savoring both Czech and international dishes. The restaurant's terrace offers an exceptional backdrop for meals, especially during warmer months.

Amenities:

Hotel U Zlaté studně provides a variety of amenities to ensure guests have a comfortable and memorable stay. These amenities may include a spa, fitness facilities, concierge services, and room service.

Historical Significance:

The hotel is housed in a historic building that dates back to the 16th century. The combination of its historic architecture and modern luxury amenities creates a unique atmosphere for guests.

Views and Location:

One of the standout features of the hotel is its elevated location, offering unparalleled views of Prague's iconic landmarks. The proximity to Prague Castle and other historical sites allows guests to explore the city's history and culture conveniently.

Personalized Service:

Hotel U Zlaté studně is known for its attentive and personalized service. The staff strives to ensure that each guest's stay is comfortable and tailored to their preferences.

Nearby Attractions:

Beyond the hotel's immediate vicinity, guests can explore Prague's attractions such as Prague Castle, Charles Bridge, Lesser Town, and the Old Town Square. The hotel's central location makes it a great starting point for sightseeing.

Romantic Getaway:

The hotel's romantic ambiance, luxurious rooms, and scenic views make it a popular choice for couples seeking a romantic getaway or a special occasion.

Reservation and Availability:

Given its popularity and limited number of rooms, it's recommended to make reservations well in advance to secure your preferred dates.

FAQ

Is English widely spoken in Prague?

Yes, English is widely spoken, especially in tourist areas, hotels, and restaurants. Many locals working in the tourism industry are proficient in English.

What currency is used in Prague?

The official currency is the Czech koruna (CZK). ATMs are widely available, and credit cards are accepted in most places.

Do I need a visa to visit Prague?

Citizens of the EU, the U.S., Canada, Australia, and several other countries do not need a visa for short stays (up to 90 days). Check visa requirements based on your nationality before traveling.

What is the best time to visit Prague?

The best time to visit Prague is during the spring (April to June) and early fall (September to October) when the weather is pleasant, and tourist crowds are relatively smaller.

How do I get around Prague?

Prague has an efficient public transportation system, including trams, buses, and a metro. Walking is also a popular way to explore the city, especially in the historic center.

What are the must-visit attractions in Prague?

Some of the must-visit attractions include Prague Castle, Charles Bridge, Old Town Square, and the Astronomical Clock. These sites offer a glimpse into Prague's rich history and culture.

Is tap water safe to drink in Prague?

Yes, tap water in Prague is generally safe to drink. You can also find bottled water in stores and restaurants.

How much should I tip in restaurants and cafes?

It's customary to leave a small tip (around 10%) for service staff at restaurants, cafes, and bars. Check the bill to see if a service charge is already included.

What is the local time zone in Prague?

Prague is in the Central European Time Zone (CET), which is UTC+1. During daylight saving time (from the last Sunday in March to the last Sunday in October), it follows Central European Summer Time (CEST), which is UTC+2.

Are there any safety concerns for tourists in Prague?

Prague is generally safe for tourists. However, be cautious of pickpocketing, especially in crowded tourist areas. Keep your belongings secure and be aware of your surroundings.

How can I explore the local cuisine in Prague?

You can explore the local cuisine by trying traditional dishes such as goulash, trdelník (chimney cake), and Czech beer. Look for local restaurants and cafes to get an authentic taste of Czech cuisine.

Can I use public transportation to get from the airport to the city center?

Yes, you can use the Airport Express bus or public buses to get from Václav Havel Airport Prague to the city center. You can also take a taxi or use ride-sharing services.

Is Wi-Fi available in public places in Prague?

Yes, many hotels, restaurants, cafes, and public places offer free Wi-Fi for visitors.

How to save money on your trip

Saving money on your trip to Prague (or any destination) requires careful planning and smart choices. Here are some tips to help you save money while enjoying your time in Prague:

Travel During Off-Peak Seasons:

Visiting during shoulder seasons (spring and fall) can result in lower airfare and accommodation prices compared to peak tourist months.

Book Flights and Accommodation in Advance:

Booking your flights and accommodation early can help you secure better deals and avoid last-minute price hikes.

Walk or Rent a Bike:

Many of Prague's attractions are within walking distance of each other. Consider walking or renting a bike to explore the city at your own pace.

Stay in Budget Accommodations:

Look for budget-friendly hostels, guesthouses, or apartment rentals that offer comfortable stays without breaking the bank.

Cook Your Own Meals:

If you have access to a kitchen, consider buying groceries and cooking some of your own meals. This can help you save on dining expenses.

Eat at Local Restaurants:

Opt for local eateries and cafes rather than touristy restaurants, as they often offer more affordable and authentic dining experiences.

Use Free or Discounted Attractions:

Take advantage of free walking tours, explore public parks, and visit attractions with discounted or free admission, such as some museums on specific days.

Purchase City Cards:

Consider buying a Prague Card, which offers free entry to many attractions, unlimited public transportation, and discounts at select restaurants and shops.

Avoid Excessive Tourist Areas:

Prices in touristy areas can be higher. Venture slightly away from the main attractions to find better deals on food and souvenirs.

Use Water Refill Stations:

Prague has numerous public water fountains where you can refill your water bottle for free, helping you save on bottled water costs.

Avoid Currency Exchange Kiosks:

Exchange money at banks or use ATMs to get a better exchange rate compared to currency exchange kiosks.

Research Happy Hours:

Many bars and restaurants offer discounted drinks and food during happy hours. Take advantage of these deals to save on your dining expenses.

Limit Guided Tours:

While guided tours can be informative, consider limiting them to a few key attractions and explore the rest on your own.

Use Cash:

Some places may offer discounts if you pay in cash. Additionally, using a credit card with no foreign transaction fees can help you save on currency conversion charges.

Use Public Transportation:

Prague has an efficient and affordable public transportation system, including trams, buses, a

nd the metro. Purchase multi-day travel passes for cost-effective commuting.

Pack Light:

Avoid excess baggage fees by packing only what you need. Pack versatile clothing items that can be mixed and matched.

Plan a Picnic:

Enjoy a budget-friendly meal by having a picnic in one of Prague's parks or scenic spots.

PRAGUE EXTENSIVE ARCHITECTURE

Prague is renowned for its extensive and diverse architecture, showcasing a rich history of various architectural styles spanning centuries. Here are some of the prominent architectural highlights you can explore in Prague:

Romanesque Architecture

Romanesque architecture is an architectural style that emerged in Europe during the 10th century and flourished throughout the 11th and 12th centuries. It is characterized by its thick walls, rounded arches, sturdy columns, and simple yet imposing designs. Romanesque architecture drew inspiration from Roman and Byzantine influences and played a significant role in shaping the architectural landscape of the medieval period. Here are some key features and examples of Romanesque architecture:

Key Features of Romanesque Architecture:

- **Thick Walls:** Romanesque buildings typically have thick walls, often constructed using stone or rubble masonry, which provided stability and durability.

- **Rounded Arches:** One of the defining features of Romanesque architecture is the widespread use of rounded arches, both in doorways and windows. These arches are often semicircular and give the structures a sense of solidity.

- **Sturdy Columns and Piers:** Romanesque buildings feature robust columns and piers that support the weight of the heavy stone structures. These columns often have simple, plain designs.

- **Small Windows:** Romanesque churches and buildings usually have small windows with rounded arches, designed for both structural integrity and defense. The small windows allowed for the retention of heat and protection from external threats.

- **Vaulted Ceilings:** Romanesque buildings often feature barrel vaults, groin vaults, or simple cross vaults, which distribute weight evenly and allow for larger, open interior spaces.

- **Decorative Elements:** While Romanesque architecture is known for its relatively simple and functional designs, some buildings feature decorative elements such as sculpted reliefs, friezes, and tympanums above doorways.

Examples of Romanesque Architecture in Prague:

- **Basilica of St. George:** Located within the Prague Castle complex, the Basilica of St. George is one of the oldest surviving churches in Prague. It features Romanesque architecture with its rounded arches and simple yet elegant design.

- **Vyšehrad Castle:** The Vyšehrad complex includes the Rotunda of St. Martin, a well-preserved Romanesque rotunda dating back to the 11th century.

- **Břevnov Monastery:** This monastery, founded in the 10th century, features a Romanesque basilica with a characteristic semicircular apse and rounded arches.

- **Old Town Bridge Tower:** While primarily Gothic in style, the Old Town Bridge Tower incorporates elements of Romanesque design, including its massive, rounded towers.

Gothic Architecture

Gothic architecture is a style that originated in the Middle Ages and is characterized by its use of pointed arches, ribbed vaults, and flying buttresses. It emerged in the 12th century and reached its height during the 13th to 15th centuries. Gothic architecture is known for its soaring verticality, intricate detailing, and the creation of spaces filled with light and symbolism. Here are some key features and examples of Gothic architecture in Prague:

Key Features of Gothic Architecture:

- **Pointed Arches:** One of the most distinctive features of Gothic architecture is the use of pointed arches, which replaced the rounded arches of Romanesque architecture. These arches created a sense of upward movement and allowed for greater height in the buildings.

- **Ribbed Vaults:** Gothic cathedrals and structures often feature ribbed vaults, which are intersecting arches that create a web-like pattern on the ceilings. Ribbed vaults provided structural support while also adding a decorative element.

- **Flying Buttresses:** Gothic buildings frequently incorporate flying buttresses, which are arched supports that extend from the exterior walls to support the weight of the walls and roof. This innovation allowed for larger windows and more open spaces.

- **Stained Glass Windows:** Gothic cathedrals are known for their magnificent stained glass windows, which were used to tell stories from the Bible and other religious narratives. The windows allowed colorful light to filter into the interior, creating a sense of awe and spirituality.

- **Vertical Emphasis:** Gothic architecture emphasizes verticality, with tall spires, pointed arches, and slender columns creating a sense of aspiration toward the heavens.

Examples of Gothic Architecture in Prague:

- **St. Vitus Cathedral:** Located within the Prague Castle complex, St. Vitus Cathedral is a masterpiece of Gothic architecture. Its soaring spires, intricate facades, and stunning stained glass windows make it one of the most iconic Gothic cathedrals in Europe.

- **Charles Bridge Towers:** The Old Town Bridge Tower and Lesser Town Bridge Tower, part of the Charles Bridge, showcase Gothic architectural elements with their pointed arches, decorative details, and statues.

- **Týn Church:** Also known as the Church of Our Lady Before Týn, this Gothic church features twin towers with spires that dominate the Old Town Square. Its interior is adorned with intricate vaulting and decorative elements.

- **Powder Tower:** The Powder Tower, originally a gate into the city, exhibits a transition from Gothic to Renaissance architecture. Its decorative details and tall spire reflect the Gothic influence.

- **Old New Synagogue:** The Old New Synagogue is one of the oldest surviving synagogues in Europe and features a Gothic design with pointed arches and ribbed vaults.

Renaissance Architecture

Renaissance architecture is a style that originated in Italy during the 14th century and spread across Europe, lasting into the 17th century. It marked a revival of classical architectural principles from ancient Greece and Rome and is characterized by its emphasis on symmetry, proportion, and the use of classical orders such as Doric, Ionic, and Corinthian columns. Renaissance architecture is known for its harmonious proportions, decorative elements, and the integration of art and architecture. Here are some key features and examples of Renaissance architecture in Prague:

Key Features of Renaissance Architecture:

- **Classical Elements:** Renaissance architecture drew inspiration from the classical architectural forms of ancient Greece and Rome. It utilized features such as columns, pilasters, pediments, and domes in its designs.

- **Symmetry and Proportion:** Renaissance buildings are characterized by their balance and symmetry. Proportions were carefully calculated to create visually pleasing and harmonious structures.

- **Humanism and Individualism:** Renaissance architecture reflected the humanist ideals of the period, emphasizing the importance of the individual and celebrating human achievements through architecture.

- **Use of Orders:** Renaissance buildings often featured columns and pilasters with classical orders, such as Doric, Ionic, and Corinthian. These orders added a sense of grandeur and sophistication to the structures.

- **Aesthetic Harmony:** Renaissance architects aimed to create buildings that were not only functional but also aesthetically pleasing. They paid attention to details such as ornamentation, sculptural elements, and decorative facades.

Examples of Renaissance Architecture in Prague:

- **Prague Castle's Royal Summer Palace:** This elegant Renaissance palace is located within the Prague Castle complex. It features decorative facades, arched windows, and symmetrical design elements.

- **Schwarzenberg Palace:** The Schwarzenberg Palace is a prime example of Renaissance architecture with its ornate facades, classical orders, and harmonious proportions.

- **Clementinum:** The Clementinum complex includes various buildings with Renaissance elements, such as the Astronomical Tower and the Baroque Library Hall. The facade of the Astronomical Tower showcases Renaissance influences.

- **St. Nicholas Church (Malá Strana):** While primarily Baroque in style, St. Nicholas Church incorporates

Renaissance features, including its dome and interior decorative elements.

- **Lobkowicz Palace:** This palace features a blend of Renaissance and Baroque architectural styles, with a focus on symmetry and decorative details.

Baroque Architecture

Baroque architecture is a style that originated in the 17th century and continued into the 18th century. It emerged as a response to the Renaissance and is characterized by its grandeur, theatricality, and elaborate ornamentation. Baroque architecture often features curving forms, dynamic movement, and a sense of drama. This style is closely associated with the Catholic Counter-Reformation, as many Baroque buildings were constructed as expressions of religious devotion and power. Here are some key features and examples of Baroque architecture in Prague:

Key Features of Baroque Architecture:

- **Dramatic and Dynamic Forms:** Baroque buildings often feature curving facades, dramatic curves, and dynamic shapes that create a sense of movement and energy.

- **Elaborate Ornamentation:** Baroque architecture is known for its rich ornamentation, including intricate sculptures, decorative details, and elaborate facades.

- **Illusionistic Techniques:** Baroque architects employed illusionistic techniques such as trompe-l'oeil (trick of the eye) to create optical illusions and give the impression of depth and three-dimensionality.

- **Use of Light and Shadow:** Baroque buildings use light and shadow to create dramatic effects, emphasizing certain architectural elements and creating a sense of depth.

- **Dramatic Interiors:** Baroque interiors often feature ornate stucco work, frescoes, and gilded decorations. These interiors are designed to create a sense of awe and wonder.

Examples of Baroque Architecture in Prague:

- **St. Nicholas Church (Malá Strana):** This grand Baroque church is characterized by its imposing dome, elaborate stucco work, and decorative elements. The interior is equally opulent, with intricate frescoes and ornate details.

- **Clementinum and Baroque Library Hall:** The Baroque Library Hall within the Clementinum complex is a masterpiece of Baroque design. Its ceiling features a stunning fresco that gives the illusion of a domed ceiling.

- **St. Nicholas Church (Old Town Square):** Another St. Nicholas Church, located in the Old Town Square, showcases Baroque features such as its ornate facade and beautifully detailed interior.

- **Church of Our Lady Victorious (Infant Jesus of Prague):** This Baroque church is famous for its statue of the Infant Jesus of Prague. The facade features Baroque elements, and the interior is adorned with lavish decoration.
- **Schwarzenberg Palace:** The palace's Baroque facade is adorned with decorative sculptures and elaborate detailing.

Rococo Architecture

Rococo architecture is an ornate and highly decorative style that emerged in the early 18th century as a continuation of the Baroque style. It is characterized by its emphasis on intricate ornamentation, delicate forms, and a sense of lightness and playfulness. Rococo architecture is often associated with luxury, elegance, and a focus on interior spaces. While it shares some similarities with Baroque architecture, Rococo places a greater emphasis on decorative details and asymmetrical design. Here are some key features and examples of Rococo architecture in Prague:

Key Features of Rococo Architecture:

- **Ornate Decorations:** Rococo architecture is known for its lavish ornamentation, including intricate stucco work, gilded details, and delicate carvings.

- **Curved Lines and Forms:** Rococo buildings often feature curving facades, scrollwork, and asymmetrical shapes that create a sense of movement and grace.

- **Pastel Colors:** Rococo interiors are often characterized by pastel color schemes, which contribute to the light and airy atmosphere of the style.

- **Focus on Interior Spaces:** Rococo places a strong emphasis on interior design, with attention to creating comfortable and elegant spaces adorned with decorative elements.

- **Natural and Organic Motifs:** Rococo often incorporates motifs inspired by nature, such as flowers, leaves, and shells, creating a sense of whimsy and fantasy.

Examples of Rococo Architecture in Prague:

- **Kinský Palace:** This Rococo palace is known for its beautifully decorated facade featuring intricate stucco work and delicate carvings. The interior rooms are adorned with ornate details and elegant furnishings.

- **Clam-Gallas Palace:** Another example of Rococo architecture, the Clam-Gallas Palace features a graceful facade with decorative elements and a sense of lightness.

- **Černín Palace:** This palace showcases a blend of Baroque and Rococo influences in its design. The Rococo elements can be seen in the interior spaces, including the ornate staircase.

- **Troja Chateau:** Located just outside Prague, Troja Chateau is a stunning example of Rococo architecture. The chateau's interior features intricate stucco work, frescoes, and elegant design.

- **Schönborn Palace:** This palace's facade features Rococo ornamentation and decorative details, contributing to the overall elegance of the building.

Art Nouveau Architecture

Art Nouveau, also known as Jugendstil or Modernisme, is an artistic and architectural style that emerged at the turn of the 20th century. It is characterized by its focus on organic and curvilinear forms, as well as its emphasis on decorative details inspired by nature. Art Nouveau architecture sought to break away from traditional design and create a harmonious integration of art and architecture. In Prague, this style is particularly prominent and has left a significant mark on the city's architectural landscape. Here are some key features and examples of Art Nouveau architecture in Prague:

Key Features of Art Nouveau Architecture:

- **Curvilinear Forms:** Art Nouveau buildings often feature flowing and sinuous lines, creating a sense of movement and organic unity.

- **Nature-Inspired Motifs:** Nature is a central theme in Art Nouveau, and buildings of this style frequently incorporate motifs such as flowers, leaves, vines, and insects in their decorations.

- **Ornate Facades:** Art Nouveau buildings are characterized by their intricately decorated facades, which may include decorative ironwork, stained glass, and ceramic tiles.

- **Asymmetry:** Art Nouveau often embraces asymmetry and avoids rigid, symmetrical designs, giving buildings a more dynamic and unconventional appearance.

- **Innovative Materials:** Architects of the Art Nouveau period experimented with new materials and techniques, including the use of cast iron, glass, and concrete.

Examples of Art Nouveau Architecture in Prague:

- **Municipal House (Obecní dům):** This iconic building is a masterpiece of Art Nouveau architecture in Prague. Its facade is adorned with decorative details, including sculptures, mosaics, and ornate ironwork.

- **House of the Black Madonna (Dům U Černé Matky Boží):** This building is home to the Czech Cubism Museum and is a prime example of Art Nouveau design. Its facade features intricate geometric patterns and decorative elements.

- **Grand Hotel Europa:** This historic hotel showcases Art Nouveau elements in its facade, with ornate details and decorative features that capture the essence of the style.

- **Villa Müller:** Designed by renowned architect Adolf Loos, Villa Müller is an example of the transition from Art Nouveau to early modernist architecture. It features elements of both styles.

- **Ruprechtov House:** This building features Art Nouveau ornamentation, including floral motifs and decorative ironwork on its facade.

- **Lucerna Palace:** The Lucerna Palace houses a variety of cultural and entertainment venues. Its Art Nouveau arcade is adorned with decorative mosaics and sculptures.

Functionalism

Functionalism, also known as the International Style or the Modern Movement, is an architectural and design philosophy that emerged in the early 20th century as a response to the changing social and technological landscape of the time. It emphasizes the idea that the form of a building or object should be primarily determined by its function or purpose, rather than relying on historical ornamentation or decorative elements. Functionalism became a significant movement in architecture, design, and urban planning, advocating for simplicity, efficiency, and a focus on practicality.

Key Principles of Functionalism:

- **Form Follows Function:** The central tenet of functionalism is that the design and form of a building or object should be determined by its intended use and purpose. Functionality takes precedence over aesthetics or decoration.

- **Minimalism:** Functionalism embraces minimalistic design, avoiding unnecessary embellishments and ornamentation. Clean lines, simple shapes, and a reduction of decorative elements are characteristic of functionalist design.

- **Technological Innovation:** Functionalism embraced advances in materials, construction methods, and technology. New materials like steel, glass, and reinforced concrete allowed for innovative architectural solutions and open floor plans.

- **Efficiency and Rationality:** Functionalism promotes efficient and rational design solutions that optimize space and functionality. Spaces are organized logically, and every element serves a specific purpose.

- **Open Floor Plans:** Buildings designed in the functionalist style often feature open and flexible interior spaces, allowing for adaptable use and easy circulation.

- **Emphasis on Light and Air:** Functionalism emphasizes the importance of natural light and ventilation in interior spaces, leading to the incorporation of large windows and open spaces.

Examples of Functionalism in Prague:

- **Villa Müller:** Designed by architect Adolf Loos, Villa Müller is a prime example of functionalist architecture. It features an open layout, flat roofs, and large windows that provide ample natural light.

- **Kotěra House:** Designed by Jan Kotěra, this building is considered one of the earliest examples of functionalism in Prague. Its facade is characterized by clean lines and geometric shapes.

- **Veletržní Palace:** This building, designed by architect Josef Fuchs, is part of the National Gallery in Prague. It showcases functionalist features, such as a modernist facade and an emphasis on efficient use of space.

- **Functionalism in Housing Estates**: Prague's functionalist housing estates, such as Baba and Hloubětín, embody the principles of functionalist urban planning, with simple and rational layouts that prioritize the needs of residents.

Contemporary Architecture

Contemporary architecture refers to the architectural styles and trends that are currently in practice and development. It encompasses a wide range of approaches, aesthetics, and design philosophies, reflecting the evolving needs, technologies, and cultural influences of the present day. Contemporary architecture is not defined by a single style but rather by the diversity and innovation of designs created in the modern era.

Key Characteristics of Contemporary Architecture:

- **Innovation:** Contemporary architecture embraces innovative design solutions, often incorporating advanced technologies and sustainable practices.

- **Sustainability:** Many contemporary architects prioritize environmentally conscious design, integrating energy-efficient systems, renewable materials, and sustainable construction techniques.

- **Functionality:** Like functionalism, contemporary architecture emphasizes the functionality and practicality of spaces, often resulting in flexible and adaptable designs.

- **Material Exploration:** Contemporary architects often experiment with a variety of materials, combining traditional and modern elements to create unique and expressive buildings.

- **Openness and Transparency:** Contemporary architecture often features open floor plans and extensive use of glass, blurring the boundaries between indoor and outdoor spaces.

- **Fluid Forms:** Contemporary buildings may exhibit fluid and organic shapes, challenging traditional rectilinear structures.

- **Cultural Context:** Many contemporary architects incorporate local and cultural influences into their designs, creating buildings that respond to their surroundings.

Examples of Contemporary Architecture in Prague:

- **Dancing House (Tančící dům):** Designed by Frank Gehry and Vlado Milunić, the Dancing House is a striking example of contemporary architecture in Prague. Its dynamic and curvilinear form stands out amidst the city's historic buildings.

- **DOX Centre for Contemporary Art:** This art museum, designed by Ivan Kroupa, features a modern and minimalist exterior, reflecting the aesthetic of contemporary art.

- **MeetFactory:** A cultural center and art gallery, MeetFactory showcases a blend of industrial and contemporary design elements, fostering creativity and experimentation.

- **Quadrio:** This mixed-use development by Ricardo Bofill features a glass facade that contributes to the modern character of the neighborhood.

- **City Empiria:** A commercial building with a distinctive, angular design, City Empiria exemplifies the diversity of contemporary architectural approaches.

- **Nová Scéna:** Designed by Karel Prager, Nová Scéna is a modern theater complex with a unique glass facade that adds a contemporary touch to the cityscape.

Cubist Architecture

Cubist architecture is a unique and innovative architectural style that emerged in the early 20th century, primarily in the Czech Republic and particularly in the city of Prague. Inspired by the Cubist art movement, which was characterized by the fragmentation and abstraction of forms, Cubist architecture sought to break away from traditional architectural conventions and create buildings with distinct geometric shapes, sharp angles, and dynamic compositions.

Key Characteristics of Cubist Architecture:

- **Geometric Forms:** Cubist buildings are characterized by their use of geometric shapes, such as cubes, pyramids, and prisms. These shapes are often fragmented and reassembled to create intricate and unconventional architectural compositions.

- **Sharp Angles and Lines:** Cubist architecture features sharp angles, lines, and facets that create a sense of dynamism and visual interest. Facades may be composed of overlapping planes that intersect at various angles.

- **Abstraction:** Similar to Cubist art, Cubist architecture seeks to abstract and reinterpret reality. Elements of the building are simplified and distilled to their essential forms.

- **Asymmetry:** Cubist buildings often exhibit asymmetrical designs, where different parts of the structure may be varied in size, shape, and placement.

- **Ornamentation:** Unlike some other modernist movements, Cubist architecture does incorporate ornamental elements, often in the form of intricate geometric patterns, which are integrated into the overall design.

- **Integration of Art and Architecture:** Cubist architects often collaborated closely with artists, including painters and sculptors, to create a unified aesthetic that extended from the building's exterior to its interior.

- **Limited Application:** Cubist architecture was primarily a Czech phenomenon, and its influence was relatively short-lived, lasting from around 1910 to the early 1920s.

Examples of Cubist Architecture in Prague:

- **House of the Black Madonna (Dům U Černé Matky Boží):** Designed by Josef Gočár, this iconic Cubist building is one of the most well-known examples of the style. It houses the Museum of Czech Cubism and features a distinctive facade with sharp angles and geometric ornamentation.

- **Cubist Buildings on Celetná Street:** Several buildings along Celetná Street in Prague showcase Cubist design elements, including the House of the Stone Bell (Dům U Kamenného zvonu) and the Rott House (Rottova palác).

- **Adria Palace:** Designed by Pavel Janák, Adria Palace is characterized by its angular facade and geometric decorative details.

- **Müller Villa (Muzeum Kampa):** Designed by Adolf Loos, the Müller Villa features Cubist-inspired elements in combination with Loos's minimalist design approach.

HIGHLIGHTS AND GEMS

Here are some of the main highlights and gems of Prague:

Prague Castle (Pražský hrad)

Prague Castle (Pražský hrad) is a historic and architectural masterpiece that sits atop a hill overlooking the city of Prague, Czech Republic. It is one of the most iconic landmarks in the country and a must-visit destination for tourists. Here's an overview of Prague Castle and what you can expect to explore:

Historical Significance:

Prague Castle has a rich history dating back over a thousand years. It was founded in the 9th century and has served as the seat of Czech kings, emperors, and presidents. The castle complex has witnessed numerous significant events in Czech and European history.

Architectural Marvel:

The castle complex is a stunning blend of various architectural styles, including Romanesque, Gothic, Renaissance, Baroque, and Rococo. The mix of styles reflects the evolution of the castle over centuries and showcases the artistic and cultural influences that shaped Prague.

Key Highlights:

- **St. Vitus Cathedral:** The centerpiece of the castle complex, this magnificent Gothic cathedral is home to the Czech Crown Jewels and the final resting place of many Bohemian kings and saints.

- **Old Royal Palace:** This historic palace features grand halls, including the Vladislav Hall, where royal ceremonies and banquets took place.

- **Golden Lane:** A charming street of colorful historic houses, once home to castle craftsmen and alchemists. Franz Kafka also lived in one of these houses.

- **Daliborka Tower:** A former prison that offers panoramic views of Prague and the surrounding area.

- **Basilica of St. George:** A Romanesque church with a beautiful interior and a convent.

- **Powder Tower:** The main entrance to the castle complex, adorned with intricate decoration.

- **Royal Garden:** A peaceful garden with beautiful landscaping, statues, and architectural elements.

- **Lobkowicz Palace:** Located nearby, this private palace is home to a renowned art collection and offers a fascinating look into the history of the Lobkowicz family.

Changing of the Guard:

A popular attraction is the Changing of the Guard ceremony, which takes place daily at the castle's main entrance. The ceremony features soldiers in traditional uniforms marching to the sound of a military band.

Panoramic Views:

The castle's elevated location provides breathtaking panoramic views of Prague and the Vltava River. It's an excellent spot for capturing memorable photographs.

Opening Hours:

The opening hours of different areas within the castle complex may vary. It's recommended to check the official website for up-to-date information.

Tickets:

Visitors can purchase tickets to access specific areas of the castle, or choose a combined ticket that includes multiple attractions.

Guided Tours: Guided tours are available and provide insights into the history, architecture, and stories behind Prague Castle.

Old Town Square (Staroměstské náměstí)

Old Town Square (Staroměstské náměstí) is the historic heart of Prague, Czech Republic, and one of the most vibrant and picturesque squares in Europe. It is surrounded by stunning architecture, colorful buildings, and a rich history. Here's an overview of Old Town Square and what you can experience when visiting:

Historical Significance:

Old Town Square dates back to the 12th century and has served as a central hub for various historical and cultural events. It has witnessed royal coronations, medieval markets, executions, and celebrations.

Architectural Marvels:

The square is surrounded by a mix of architectural styles, including Gothic, Baroque, and Renaissance. Some of the key buildings and landmarks include:

Key Highlights:

- **Church of Our Lady before Týn:** A magnificent Gothic church with striking twin spires that dominate the skyline.
- **Old Town Hall:** The iconic tower features the Prague Astronomical Clock, a medieval marvel that displays the time, astronomical information, and various figurines.

- **St. Nicholas Church:** A Baroque masterpiece with a stunning interior and a dome that offers panoramic views of the city.
- **Kinský Palace:** A Rococo palace known for its intricate façade and artistic details.

Jan Hus Memorial:

In the center of the square stands the Jan Hus Memorial, a monument dedicated to the Czech religious reformer. It serves as a symbol of Czech nationalism and resistance.

Vibrant Atmosphere:

Old Town Square is always bustling with activity. It's a gathering place for tourists and locals alike. You'll find street performers, artists, market stalls, and outdoor cafes contributing to the lively ambiance.

Seasonal Markets and Events:

Throughout the year, the square hosts various markets and events, including the famous Christmas markets with traditional crafts, mulled wine, and holiday decorations.

Cultural Hub:

The square is not only a historic site but also a cultural hub. It often hosts concerts, exhibitions, and festivals, making it a vibrant destination for art and entertainment.

Astronomical Clock (Pražský orloj)

The Prague Astronomical Clock (Pražský orloj) is one of the most famous and iconic landmarks in Prague, Czech Republic. It is a magnificent medieval astronomical clock that dates back to the 15th century and is located on the southern wall of the Old Town Hall in the Old Town Square. Here's an overview of the Prague Astronomical Clock and its fascinating features:

Historical Significance:

The Prague Astronomical Clock was installed in 1410, making it one of the oldest astronomical clocks still in operation. It was created by clockmaker Mikuláš of Kadaň and astronomer Jan Šindel, with the intention of providing citizens with information about time, astronomical events, and religious symbolism.

Astronomical Functions:

The clock is a complex mechanical device that features several components, including an astronomical dial that displays various astronomical and astrological information:

Key Highlights:

- **The Moving Clockwork:** The outer ring of the clock shows the 24-hour time cycle, with Roman numerals and a single hand.
- **The Zodiac Ring:** This rotating ring features the twelve zodiac signs and provides information about the position of the Sun within each sign.
- **The Sun and Moon:** Two small windows depict the position of the Sun and the Moon in the sky.
- **The Earth and Moon:** The lower part of the clock shows a representation of the Earth and the Moon, with the Moon's phases indicated.
- **The Walk of the Apostles:** Every hour, a fascinating spectacle known as "The Walk of the Apostles" takes place. Twelve apostolic figures appear at the windows above the astronomical dial, while the skeleton of Death strikes the time on a bell. This procession of apostles is accompanied by music and rotating figurines.

Cultural and Symbolic Elements:

The clock is adorned with intricate decorations and symbolic details that reflect the medieval understanding of the cosmos and the role of time. It features allegorical representations of the four elements (earth, water, air, fire), as well as depictions of vanity and the transience of life.

Tourist Attraction:

The Prague Astronomical Clock is a major tourist attraction and a gathering point in the Old Town Square. Visitors from around the world gather in front of the clock to witness the hourly performance of "The Walk of the Apostles" and marvel at the clock's intricate design.

Josefov (Jewish Quarter)

Josefov, also known as the Jewish Quarter, is a historic and culturally significant neighborhood located in the heart of Prague, Czech Republic. It is renowned for its rich Jewish heritage, architectural landmarks, and deep historical connections. Here's an overview of Josefov and what you can explore when visiting:

Historical Significance:

Josefov has a long and storied history dating back to the 13th century when it was established as a segregated Jewish ghetto. Over the centuries, the Jewish community faced periods of discrimination and persecution, but it also thrived culturally and economically. Today, Josefov stands as a testament to the resilience and contributions of Prague's Jewish population.

Old-New Synagogue (Staronová synagoga):

The oldest active synagogue in Europe, known for its Gothic architecture and storied history.

Spanish Synagogue (Španělská synagoga):

An exquisitely designed synagogue showcasing a mix of Moorish and Art Nouveau elements.

Klausen Synagogue (Klausová synagoga):

Part of the Jewish Museum in Prague, it houses an exhibition on the Jewish customs and lifecycle.

Jewish Cemetery:

The Jewish Cemetery is a poignant and evocative site within Josefov. Due to limited space, graves are stacked on top of each other, creating a unique and visually striking landscape. Notable figures, including Rabbi Judah Loew ben Bezalel (the legendary Golem creator), are buried here.

Jewish Museum:

The Jewish Museum in Prague consists of several historical sites, including synagogues, a ceremonial hall, and the aforementioned cemetery. It offers insights into the history, culture, and traditions of the Jewish community in Prague.

Memorials and Monuments:

Throughout Josefov, you'll find memorials and monuments dedicated to the victims of the Holocaust, honoring those who perished during World War II. One notable memorial is the Pinkas Synagogue, which displays the names of over 77,000 Czech and Moravian Holocaust victims.

Franz Kafka Connection:

Josefov was the birthplace of renowned writer Franz Kafka, and his legacy is still celebrated in the neighborhood. The Franz Kafka Monument and the Franz Kafka Museum are dedicated to his life and work.

Cultural Events:

Josefov hosts various cultural events, exhibitions, and festivals that celebrate Jewish heritage and art. These events provide a unique opportunity to engage with the neighborhood's cultural vibrancy.

Petřín Hill

Petřín Hill, often referred to as the "Green Heart of Prague," is a picturesque hill located in the heart of Prague, Czech Republic. It offers a peaceful escape from the bustling city streets and provides stunning panoramic views of Prague's iconic skyline. Here's what you need to know about Petřín Hill:

Natural Beauty:

Petřín Hill is known for its lush greenery, gardens, and serene atmosphere. It is a popular spot for both locals and tourists to enjoy leisurely walks, picnics, and relaxation amidst nature.

Petřín Lookout Tower:

The most iconic feature of Petřín Hill is the Petřín Lookout Tower (Petřínská rozhledna), often referred to as Prague's "Little Eiffel Tower." This 63-meter-tall tower was built in 1891 and offers panoramic views of Prague from its observation deck. Visitors can climb the tower's spiral staircase or take an elevator to the top for breathtaking vistas of the city, including Prague Castle, Charles Bridge, and the Vltava River.

Mirror Maze and Observatory:

Adjacent to the Petřín Lookout Tower is the Petřín Mirror Maze, a fun and quirky attraction where visitors can navigate through a maze of mirrors and glass panels. The adjacent Stefanik Observatory is also worth a visit, allowing visitors to observe the night sky through telescopes.

Labyrinths and Gardens:

Petřín Hill features several beautifully landscaped gardens, walking paths, and labyrinths. The Rose Garden (Růžová zahrada) is particularly popular in the summer months when its colorful blooms are in full display.

Petřín Funicular:

To reach the top of Petřín Hill, visitors can take the Petřín Funicular, a charming cable railway that provides a convenient and scenic ride. The funicular journey itself is a delightful experience.

Memorial to the Victims of Communism:

At the base of Petřín Hill, near the Ujezd tram station, you'll find the Memorial to the Victims of Communism. This somber monument pays tribute to those who suffered under Czechoslovakia's communist regime.

Picnic and Relaxation:

Petřín Hill is an ideal place to unwind and enjoy a leisurely picnic. Its tranquil setting and stunning views make it a favorite spot for both locals and tourists to escape the city's hustle and bustle.

Vyšehrad

Vyšehrad is a historic fortress and district located on a hill overlooking the Vltava River in Prague, Czech Republic. It holds significant historical and cultural importance and is often visited by tourists seeking to explore Prague's rich heritage. Here's an overview of Vyšehrad and its main attractions:

Historical Significance:

Vyšehrad has a history dating back to the 10th century and is often associated with the legendary origins of Prague. It was once a royal residence, fortress, and seat of power for Czech rulers. Over the centuries, Vyšehrad has witnessed important events in Czech history and has become a symbol of Czech national pride.

Vyšehrad Castle:

While not as well-known as Prague Castle, Vyšehrad Castle (Hrad Vyšehrad) is a historic complex that includes remnants of medieval fortifications, a Romanesque-style rotunda, and the neo-Gothic Church of St. Peter and St. Paul. The church's twin spires are a prominent feature of Prague's skyline. The Vyšehrad Cemetery is also located within the castle grounds and serves as the final resting place for many notable Czech figures.

St. Martin Rotunda:

The St. Martin Rotunda is one of the oldest extant buildings in Prague. It is a round Romanesque rotunda that dates back to the 11th century. The rotunda features well-preserved frescoes from the 12th century and is a fascinating example of medieval architecture.

Devil's Column and Legends:

A column known as the Devil's Column (Čertovský sloup) stands near the St. Martin Rotunda. According to legend, it marks the spot where the devil tried to thwart the construction of the rotunda by misplacing building materials each night.

Gardens and Parks:

Vyšehrad is surrounded by beautifully landscaped gardens and parks, offering a peaceful and scenic retreat. The Vyšehrad Park is a popular place for both locals and visitors to relax, take leisurely walks, and enjoy views of the river and city.

Vyšehrad Cemetery:

The Vyšehrad Cemetery is the final resting place for many notable Czech figures, including composers, writers, artists, and political leaders. It is a serene and contemplative place to explore and pay respects.

Cultural Events and Festivals:

Throughout the year, Vyšehrad hosts various cultural events, concerts, and festivals. These events showcase Czech traditions, music, and arts, making it an excellent opportunity to immerse yourself in the local culture.

Panoramic Views:

Vyšehrad offers stunning panoramic views of Prague, especially from its elevated position overlooking the Vltava River. The vantage point provides excellent photo opportunities, particularly during sunrise or sunset.

Dancing House (Tančící dům)

The Dancing House, known as "Tančící dům" in Czech, is one of Prague's most iconic and distinctive modern architectural landmarks. Also referred to as the "Fred and Ginger Building," the Dancing House stands out for its unique and playful design. Here's what you need to know about this architectural gem:

Architectural Design:

The Dancing House was designed by renowned architects Vlado Milunić and Frank Gehry. It was completed in 1996 and stands as a testament to contemporary architecture's ability to contrast with Prague's historic surroundings. The building's design evokes the image of a dancing couple, with one tower resembling a woman (Ginger Rogers) and the other a man (Fred Astaire).

Curved Forms and Twisting Facades:

The most distinctive feature of the Dancing House is its unconventional, curvaceous form. The façade appears to twist and dance, creating a dynamic visual effect that sets it apart from the surrounding buildings. The undulating lines and flowing shapes are a departure from traditional architectural norms and make the building a true work of art.

Glass and Concrete:

The Dancing House's facade is composed of glass panels and concrete elements, which further emphasize its modern aesthetic. The use of glass allows for ample natural light to enter the building's interior spaces and provides stunning views of the Vltava River and the Prague Castle across the river.

Functionality:

The Dancing House is a multifunctional building, housing office spaces, a restaurant, and a bar. The restaurant, called "Ginger & Fred," offers panoramic views of the city and is a popular spot for both locals and tourists to enjoy a meal while taking in the unique architecture.

Contrast and Controversy:

The Dancing House's design sparked controversy when it was first proposed and constructed. Some locals initially found its modern and unconventional appearance to be in stark contrast with Prague's historic architecture. However, over time, the building has become an accepted and celebrated part of the city's urban landscape.

Location:

The Dancing House is situated on the Rašínovo nábřeží (Rašín Embankment) along the Vltava River, near the Jirásek Bridge. Its central location makes it easily accessible and a convenient stop for visitors exploring the city.

Photography and Observation:

The Dancing House is a popular subject for photographers due to its unique design. Visitors can capture stunning shots of the building from various angles, both during the day and when illuminated at night.

Lennon Wall

The Lennon Wall, located in Prague, Czech Republic, is a symbolic and colorful piece of street art that pays tribute to John Lennon and promotes messages of peace and freedom. Here's what you need to know about this unique and culturally significant landmark:

Origin and History:

The Lennon Wall emerged in the 1980s as a form of peaceful protest against the Communist regime in Czechoslovakia. Inspired by John Lennon's music and his messages of love and peace, young Czechs began painting Beatles lyrics, quotes, and portraits of Lennon on a wall located near the Knights of Malta Garden, across from the French Embassy.

Role in Czech History:

During the Communist era, Western pop culture and music, including that of the Beatles, were frowned upon by the authorities. The act of expressing oneself through the Lennon Wall became a way for young people to voice their desire for freedom, democracy, and cultural openness.

Symbolism and Evolution:

Over the years, the wall has evolved and transformed into a constantly changing canvas of graffiti, artwork, and messages from people all over the world. It has become a symbol of free expression, hope, and unity. The vibrant and dynamic nature of the wall reflects the spirit of the people and the power of art as a means of communication.

Visiting the Lennon Wall:

The Lennon Wall is located in the Lesser Town (Malá Strana) of Prague, near Charles Bridge. It is easily accessible and often draws a crowd of visitors and art enthusiasts. While the wall itself is a significant attraction, the surrounding area offers picturesque views of the Vltava River and Prague Castle.

Contributing to the Wall:

Visitors are welcome to contribute to the Lennon Wall by adding their own graffiti, messages, or artwork. Painting on the wall is an act of creative expression, and many people leave their mark as a way to connect with the spirit of the place.

Events and Celebrations:

The Lennon Wall continues to be a symbol of hope and solidarity. Various events, performances, and gatherings take place at the wall, especially on important anniversaries or occasions related to peace and activism.

Klementinum Library

The Klementinum Library, located in Prague, Czech Republic, is a stunning and historic library that is renowned for its architectural beauty and rich collection of rare and valuable books. Here's what you need to know about this remarkable library:

History and Origins:

The Klementinum Library is part of the Klementinum complex, which was originally established as a Jesuit college in the 17th century. The library itself was founded in the mid-18th century and served as the main library for the Jesuit Order's education and research activities.

Baroque Architecture:

The library is a prime example of Baroque architecture and design. Its interior features elaborate decorative elements, including intricate frescoes, gilded stucco work, and ornate wooden bookcases. The overall design creates a harmonious and grand atmosphere that reflects the opulence of the Baroque era.

Frescoes and Ceiling Art:

One of the most impressive features of the library is its stunning ceiling frescoes. The frescoes were painted by Jan Hiebl and depict allegorical and biblical themes, celebrating knowledge, wisdom, and the pursuit of learning. The vivid colors and detailed artwork contribute to the library's unique and awe-inspiring ambiance.

Historic Collection:

The Klementinum Library houses a remarkable collection of over 20,000 books, many of which are rare and valuable. The collection includes works in various fields such as theology, philosophy, science, and the arts. Some of the books date back centuries, offering insights into the intellectual pursuits of past generations.

Baroque Hall and Astronomical Tower:

In addition to the library, the Klementinum complex also includes the Baroque Hall, which was used for ceremonial gatherings and lectures. The Astronomical Tower is another highlight, offering panoramic views of Prague's Old Town and its stunning architecture.

Guided Tours:

Visitors to the Klementinum Library can explore the interior as part of guided tours. These tours provide historical context, insights into the library's architecture, and the opportunity to marvel at the magnificent frescoes and design elements.

Strahov Monastery

The Strahov Monastery is a historic religious complex located in Prague, Czech Republic. Known for its significant role in Czech history and its impressive architecture, the monastery is a popular attraction for visitors. Here's what you need to know about the Strahov Monastery:

History and Background:

The Strahov Monastery, officially known as the Royal Canonry of Premonstratensians at Strahov, was founded in 1143 by Bishop Jindřich Zdík and Vladislav II, the king of Bohemia. It is one of the oldest monasteries in Prague and has played a crucial role in the country's religious and cultural development.

Architectural Highlights:

The monastery complex features a blend of architectural styles, including Romanesque and Baroque elements. Visitors can admire the stunning façades, intricate frescoes, and ornate decorations that adorn the monastery's buildings. The library, church, and other structures showcase the craftsmanship and artistic achievements of various periods.

Strahov Library:

The Strahov Monastery is particularly famous for its two remarkable libraries: the Theological Hall and the Philosophical Hall. The libraries house an extensive collection of rare manuscripts, books, and artworks. The Theological Hall is known for its grand Baroque design and ceiling frescoes, while the Philosophical Hall boasts stunning stucco decorations and a unique illusionist ceiling painting.

Church of the Assumption of Our Lady:

The monastery's church, the Church of the Assumption of Our Lady, is a stunning example of Baroque architecture. Its interior is adorned with rich ornamentation, gilded details, and exquisite artwork. The church is still actively used for religious services.

Strahov Picture Gallery:

The Strahov Monastery also houses an art gallery with a collection of European paintings spanning from the Gothic period to the Baroque era. Visitors can appreciate works by notable artists such as Lucas Cranach the Elder, Peter Paul Rubens, and Diego Velázquez.

Gardens and Views:

The monastery grounds offer beautiful gardens and scenic viewpoints where visitors can enjoy panoramic views of Prague and the surrounding areas. The peaceful ambiance and well-maintained grounds make it a pleasant place to stroll and relax.

Visitor Information:

The monastery is located in the Strahov district of Prague, not far from Prague Castle. Guided tours are available for visitors interested in exploring the monastery's history, architecture, and collections. It's advisable to check the opening hours and any entry requirements before your visit.

Náplavka Riverbank

Náplavka Riverbank, often simply referred to as Náplavka, is a vibrant and popular area located along the Vltava River in Prague, Czech Republic. It has become a hub for cultural, social, and recreational activities, attracting both locals and visitors. Here's what you can expect to experience at Náplavka Riverbank:

Riverside Promenade:

Náplavka features a scenic riverside promenade that is perfect for leisurely strolls and enjoying picturesque views of the Vltava River and Prague's iconic landmarks. The area is especially enchanting during sunset and offers a tranquil escape from the bustling city.

Outdoor Markets:

Throughout the year, Náplavka hosts various outdoor markets, including farmers' markets, craft fairs, and flea markets. These markets offer a diverse range of products, from fresh produce and local foods to handmade crafts and vintage items. It's a great place to discover unique souvenirs and experience the local culture.

Boat Rides and Cruises:

From Náplavka, you can find boat operators offering river cruises and sightseeing tours along the Vltava River. Taking a boat ride allows you to see Prague's landmarks from a different perspective and provides a relaxing way to explore the city.

Cultural Events and Festivals:

Náplavka is a hub of cultural activities and events. Throughout the year, you can find live music performances, open-air film screenings, art exhibitions, and themed festivals taking place along the riverbank. The vibrant atmosphere makes it a lively spot for entertainment and relaxation.

Restaurants and Cafés:

The riverbank is lined with a variety of restaurants, cafés, and bars where you can enjoy a meal or a drink with a view of the river. Whether you're looking for traditional Czech cuisine or international flavors, there are plenty of options to choose from.

Relaxation and Recreation:

Locals and tourists alike enjoy spending time at Náplavka for relaxation and recreation. You'll often see people sitting by the riverbank, picnicking, playing musical instruments, or simply soaking in the atmosphere. The area provides a peaceful escape in the heart of the city.

Local Community and Social Scene:

Náplavka has a strong sense of community, and it's a place where locals gather to socialize, meet friends, and enjoy various activities. The vibrant atmosphere and friendly interactions make it a welcoming space for everyone.

Getting There:

Náplavka is easily accessible by walking from Prague's city center and major attractions. You can also use public transportation, including trams and buses, to reach the area.

Wenceslas Square

Wenceslas Square (Václavské náměstí) is one of the most famous and historically significant squares in Prague, Czech Republic. Located in the heart of the city, it has played a central role in the country's history, witnessed important events, and remains a focal point for both locals and visitors. Here's what you should know about Wenceslas Square:

Historical Significance:

Wenceslas Square has a rich history dating back to the Middle Ages. It was originally established as a horse market and has since evolved into a symbolic and cultural center. The square has been the site of many significant historical events, including protests, celebrations, and demonstrations.

Architecture and Design:

The square features a wide boulevard lined with historical buildings, shops, restaurants, and hotels. The architecture is a mix of different styles, ranging from Neo-Renaissance and Art Nouveau to modern designs. One of the prominent features is the grand statue of Saint Wenceslas on horseback, a national symbol and the patron saint of the Czech Republic.

Cultural and Commercial Hub:

Wenceslas Square is not just a historic site; it's also a vibrant cultural and commercial hub. You'll find theaters, cinemas, galleries, and museums in the area, making it a popular destination for arts and entertainment. The square is also surrounded by shops, boutiques, and department stores, making it a prime shopping district.

Monuments and Landmarks:

Aside from the statue of Saint Wenceslas, the square is home to several other monuments and landmarks. The National Museum, located at the top of the square, is an imposing Neo-Renaissance building that houses extensive collections of art, history, and natural science. The statue of King Wenceslas and the Jan Palach Memorial are also noteworthy features.

Events and Festivals:

Wenceslas Square remains a venue for various events, festivals, and gatherings. It has been the backdrop for historical speeches and celebrations, as well as modern events such as New Year's Eve celebrations, concerts, and cultural festivals.

Accessibility:

Wenceslas Square is easily accessible by public transportation, including trams and the Prague Metro. It's also within walking distance from other major attractions in the city center, making it a convenient starting point for exploring Prague.

Local Scene:

The square is frequented by both tourists and locals, and it's a common meeting point for gatherings, protests, and social activities. It offers a lively atmosphere and a glimpse into the daily life of Prague's residents.

Catacombs

Prague does not have a network of catacombs similar to those found in some other European cities like Paris or Rome. However, there are some underground areas and tunnels beneath the city that you might find intriguing:

Vyšehrad Casemates and Cellars:

Vyšehrad, a historic fortress overlooking the Vltava River, has a system of casemates and cellars that were used for defensive purposes. These underground passages and chambers offer a glimpse into the city's military history.

Prague Castle Underground:

While not exactly catacombs, Prague Castle has its own network of underground areas, including cellars and chambers. Guided tours of the castle complex often include visits to these underground spaces, revealing the castle's architectural and historical layers.

Old Town Hall Cellars:

The Old Town Hall in Prague's Old Town Square has a system of medieval cellars that were once used for storage. Some of these cellars are accessible to visitors, and guided tours may provide insight into the history of the building and the area.

Pilsner Urquell Brewery Tour:

Although not in Prague itself, a trip to the Pilsner Urquell Brewery in Pilsen (Plzeň) offers a chance to explore underground cellars where the famous Pilsner beer is brewed and stored.

Franz Kafka's Prague

Franz Kafka, one of the most influential writers of the 20th century, was born in Prague in 1883. The city had a significant impact on Kafka's life and works, and his connection to Prague is still felt today. Here's a guide to exploring Franz Kafka's Prague:

Kafka's Birthplace:

Start your exploration by visiting Franz Kafka's birthplace, located at Náměstí Franze Kafky (Franz Kafka Square) in the Old Town. The building where Kafka was born has a plaque commemorating his birth.

Kafka Museum:

The Franz Kafka Museum, located near Charles Bridge, is a must-visit for anyone interested in the writer's life and works. The museum features a collection of Kafka's letters, diaries, manuscripts, and personal belongings. It provides insights into his literary achievements and the context in which he lived.

Kafka's Residence:

Visit the former residence of the Kafka family, known as the Kafka House. While the original building no longer stands, there is a historical marker at the site where it once stood, at the corner of Maiselova and Kaprova streets.

The Spanish Synagogue:

The Spanish Synagogue, part of the Jewish Museum in Prague, is a beautiful Moorish-style synagogue. Kafka often attended services here, and the synagogue is a reminder of his Jewish heritage and upbringing.

Prague's Jewish Quarter:

Explore Prague's Jewish Quarter (Josefov), where Kafka spent much of his life. Visit the Old Jewish Cemetery, the Maisel Synagogue, and the Pinkas Synagogue, which now serves as a memorial to Holocaust victims.

Café Louvre:

Café Louvre is a historic café where Kafka and other intellectuals used to gather. It's a great place to enjoy a coffee and immerse yourself in the literary atmosphere.

Charles Bridge:

Walk across Charles Bridge, which features prominently in Kafka's stories. The bridge and its surroundings are mentioned in his work "The Bridge."

Old Town Square:

Stroll through the Old Town Square, where Kafka often walked and observed the bustling city life. The square is surrounded by stunning architecture and is a central part of Kafka's Prague.

Wenceslas Square:

While not directly associated with Kafka's works, Wenceslas Square was a significant location in his life and the city's history. It's a vibrant area and an integral part of Prague's cultural scene.

Kafka Walking Tours:

Consider joining a Kafka-themed walking tour that will take you to the key sites associated with the writer. These tours provide in-depth insights into Kafka's life, works, and his relationship with the city.

Municipal Library of Prague

The Municipal Library of Prague, also known as the "Městská knihovna v Praze" in Czech, is a significant cultural institution located in the heart of Prague, Czech Republic. It's not only a library but also a hub for various cultural and educational activities. Here's a brief guide to help you explore the Municipal Library of Prague:

Location:

The Municipal Library of Prague is situated in the historical center of Prague, near the famous Wenceslas Square. The exact address is Mariánské náměstí 1, 110 00 Prague 1.

Architecture and Design:

The library building is an architectural masterpiece that blends modern design with historic elements. It was designed by the well-known Czech architect Jan Kaplický and completed in 2001. The most striking feature is the "Eye" - a large, futuristic, mirrored dome that serves as the main entrance. The interior spaces are open and contemporary, providing an inviting atmosphere for visitors.

Collections:

The Municipal Library of Prague offers a diverse range of materials, including books, magazines, newspapers, and multimedia resources. The library's collections cover various fields, including literature, history, arts, sciences, and more. They have materials available in both Czech and other languages.

Services:

Apart from traditional library services, the Municipal Library offers a range of modern amenities to cater to the needs of visitors. These include free Wi-Fi, computer stations, study areas, and meeting rooms.

Cultural Events:

The library plays a significant role in promoting cultural and educational activities. It hosts numerous events, such as author talks, book launches, workshops, exhibitions, and concerts. These events provide an opportunity for locals and tourists to engage with Czech culture and art.

Special Collections and Exhibitions:

The library often curates special exhibitions that showcase unique items from their collections. These exhibitions can cover various themes, such as historical artifacts, rare books, and contemporary art installations.

Café and Bookstore:

The library features a café where visitors can relax, enjoy a cup of coffee, and read books or work on their laptops. Additionally, there is a bookstore where you can purchase books, souvenirs, and other items related to Czech culture and literature.

Accessibility:

The Municipal Library of Prague is easily accessible by public transportation. The closest metro station is "Můstek," which is served by lines A and B. Tram stops and bus stops are also within walking distance.

Opening Hours:

Opening hours may vary, so it's recommended to check the library's official website for the most up-to-date information on operating hours.

Admission:

Entry to the library is generally free, but there might be charges for specific events, exhibitions, or services.

Olsany cemetry

The Olšany Cemetery (Olšanské hřbitovy) is one of the largest and most significant cemeteries in Prague, Czech Republic. It is located in the Žižkov district and holds historical, cultural, and artistic importance. Here's an overview of the Olšany Cemetery:

Location:

The Olšany Cemetery is situated in the Žižkov district of Prague. The main entrance is located at Vinohradská cesta 1535/5, 130 00 Prague 3. It's easily accessible by public transportation, making it a notable destination for visitors.

Historical Significance:

Established in the late 19th century, the Olšany Cemetery holds a rich history and serves as the final resting place for many prominent Czech figures. It became one of the most prestigious cemeteries in Prague due to its historical and cultural significance.

Architectural and Artistic Features:

The cemetery is not only a burial ground but also a place of artistic and architectural interest. It features a wide range of tombstones, mausoleums, and sculptures designed by renowned artists. The diversity of architectural styles reflects the changing artistic trends over the years.

Graves of Prominent Individuals:

The Olšany Cemetery is the resting place of numerous notable individuals from Czech history, including writers, artists, musicians, politicians, and public figures. Among the well-known figures buried here are Franz Kafka's family members, Karel Čapek, Jan Palach, and many others.

Sections and Religious Diversity:

The cemetery is divided into different sections, including sections for different religious and cultural groups. This reflects the diverse makeup of the city's population and the respect for various burial traditions.

Memorial Sites:

The cemetery also contains memorial sites dedicated to historical events and figures. One of the most significant is the memorial for the victims of communism, commemorating those who suffered under the Communist regime.

Visiting and Atmosphere:

The Olšany Cemetery is not only a place for honoring the deceased but also a serene space for contemplation and reflection. The atmosphere is peaceful and respectful, making it a suitable place for quiet walks and paying respects to those who have passed away.

Open to the Public:

The cemetery is open to the public, allowing visitors to explore its paths, admire the artistic elements, and pay their respects. It's a place where history, culture, and art converge.

Accessibility:

As mentioned earlier, the Olšany Cemetery is easily accessible by public transportation. The Prague Metro Line A has a station nearby, and tram stops are also in the vicinity.

Opening Hours:

The opening hours of the cemetery may vary, so it's advisable to check the official website or contact the cemetery administration for up-to-date information before planning your visit.

CULTURE

Prague, the capital city of the Czech Republic, is renowned for its rich history, stunning architecture, and vibrant cultural scene. Here's a travel guide to help you explore the cultural aspects of this beautiful city:

Performing Arts

Prague has a vibrant performing arts scene that encompasses a wide range of genres, from classical music and opera to theater and contemporary dance. Here are some key highlights and venues to explore in the realm of performing arts in Prague:

Prague National Theatre (Národní divadlo):

This historic and grand theater is a symbol of Czech national pride. It hosts opera, ballet, drama, and classical music performances. The ornate interior and exceptional acoustics make it a must-visit for any performing arts enthusiast.

Estates Theatre (Stavovské divadlo):

Built in the late 18th century, this Neo-Classical theater is famous for hosting the premiere of Mozart's opera "Don Giovanni." It continues to stage opera and ballet performances, often featuring works by classical composers.

Black Light Theatre:

Prague is known for its unique black light theater performances. These shows blend visual effects, mime, dance, and music to create captivating and surreal experiences. Some popular black light theaters in Prague include Ta Fantastika and Image Theatre.

Czech Philharmonic Orchestra (Česká filharmonie):

Experience world-class orchestral performances at the Rudolfinum, a beautiful Neo-Renaissance concert hall located along the Vltava River. The orchestra's repertoire includes classical and contemporary compositions.

Jazz and Contemporary Music:

Prague has a lively jazz scene with various clubs hosting performances by local and international jazz musicians. Venues like Jazz Dock and Agharta Jazz Centrum offer excellent jazz experiences. Additionally, you can find a variety of contemporary music concerts spanning genres from rock to electronic.

Dance Performances:

Prague hosts a range of dance performances, from traditional ballet to contemporary dance. The National Theatre and other venues often feature ballet productions, while contemporary dance can be experienced at spaces like Ponec Theatre and Archa Theatre.

Folklore and Traditional Performances:

For a taste of Czech folklore and traditional performing arts, consider attending folk dance shows or performances featuring traditional music and costumes. These shows often provide insights into Czech cultural heritage.

Film Festivals:

While not a traditional performing art, film festivals are an important part of Prague's cultural landscape. The Prague International Film Festival (Febiofest) and the One World International Human Rights Documentary Film Festival showcase a diverse range of films from around the world.

Music and Festivals

Prague is a city deeply rooted in music and is known for its rich musical heritage. From classical concerts in historic venues to lively music festivals, there's something for every music enthusiast. Here are some of the music and festivals you can experience in Prague:

Prague Spring International Music Festival:

Held annually from May to June, this prestigious classical music festival attracts renowned orchestras, conductors, and soloists from around the world. The festival showcases a diverse program of symphonic concerts, chamber music performances, and recitals.

Czech Philharmonic Orchestra:

Attending a performance by the Czech Philharmonic Orchestra at the beautiful Rudolfinum concert hall is a must for classical music lovers. The orchestra is known for its exceptional interpretations of Czech and international repertoire.

Prague Symphony Orchestra:

This orchestra offers a wide range of concerts, including classical, film music, and crossover performances, providing a diverse musical experience.

Strings of Autumn Festival:

An annual international music festival featuring a mix of classical, jazz, and world music performances. The festival often invites renowned artists and ensembles to perform in various Prague venues.

Prague Folklore Days:

Experience Czech and international folk music, dance, and traditions during this lively festival. It's a great opportunity to immerse yourself in the cultural heritage of the region.

Prague International Organ Festival:

If you appreciate organ music, don't miss this festival, which takes place in various historic churches across Prague. The performances showcase the city's impressive collection of pipe organs.

Metronome Festival:

A modern music festival featuring a lineup of international and local artists from various genres, including rock, pop, electronic, and hip-hop. The festival takes place at Výstaviště exhibition grounds.

United Islands of Prague:

A multi-genre music festival held on several islands along the Vltava River. It features live music performances, workshops, and activities, showcasing emerging and established artists.

Prague Opera and Ballet Performances:

Prague's opera houses, including the National Theatre and the State Opera, regularly host opera and ballet productions, ranging from classic to contemporary works.

Live Music Venues:

Explore Prague's vibrant live music scene by visiting clubs and venues like Jazz Dock, Lucerna Music Bar, and Roxy, where you can enjoy a variety of musical genres.

Cuisine

Prague's cuisine reflects its history and cultural influences, with a mix of traditional Czech dishes, international flavors, and modern twists. Here are some key elements of Prague's cuisine and popular dishes you should try:

Traditional Czech Dishes:

- **Svíčková:** Marinated beef served with a creamy sauce, bread dumplings, and cranberry sauce.
- **Guláš:** A hearty stew made with tender meat, typically beef or pork, cooked with onions, paprika, and other spices.

- **Knedlo, vepřo, zelo:** Roast pork with dumplings and sauerkraut, a classic Czech comfort food.
- **Utopenci:** Pickled sausages served as a snack or appetizer.
- **Vepřová kýta:** Breaded and fried pork schnitzel.
- **Tvarohovník:** A sweet dessert made from cottage cheese and topped with fruits or jam.

Street Food and Snacks:

- **Trdelník:** A sweet pastry made by wrapping dough around a cylinder, grilling it, and then dusting it with sugar and nuts.
- **Párek v rohlíku:** A Czech-style hot dog, typically served in a roll with mustard and ketchup.
- **Chlebíčky:** Open-faced sandwiches adorned with various toppings, often served as appetizers.

Soups:

- **Svíčková Soup:** A creamy soup made with the same ingredients as svíčková, featuring marinated beef and vegetables.
- **Bramborová Polévka:** Potato soup often flavored with mushrooms, garlic, and caraway seeds.

Desserts:

- **Medovník:** A honey cake made with layers of sponge cake and sweet filling, often served with whipped cream.
- **Koláče:** Fruit-filled pastries, both sweet and savory.
- **Rohlik:** A croissant-like pastry often enjoyed for breakfast or as a snack.

Beer Culture:

- **Pilsner Urquell:** The original Pilsner beer, known for its refreshing taste, is a must-try in Prague.
- **Czech Beer Varieties:** Beyond Pilsner, explore various Czech beer styles, including dark lagers and wheat beers.

International and Modern Cuisine:

- **International Restaurants:** Prague offers a diverse range of international restaurants, including Italian, Asian, Middle Eastern, and more.
- **Modern Czech Cuisine:** Some restaurants blend traditional Czech ingredients with modern techniques and presentation, offering a unique dining experience.

Cafés and Pastries:

- **Café Culture:** Explore Prague's charming cafés, where you can enjoy coffee, tea, and a variety of pastries and desserts.

- **Czech Pastries:** In addition to trdelník, try other Czech pastries like buchty (sweet buns) and kolache.

Prague's Beer Culture

Prague is renowned for its rich beer culture, and it's no exaggeration to say that beer is an integral part of the city's social fabric and history. Here's a closer look at Prague's beer culture and what you can expect to experience:

Pilsner Urquell and Czech Beer Styles:

Pilsner Urquell, one of the world's first pale lagers, was born in the Czech city of Plzeň (Pilsen). It revolutionized brewing techniques and set the standard for the crisp, golden lagers that are popular worldwide. Czech Republic boasts a wide variety of beer styles, including pale lagers (světlý ležák), dark lagers (tmavý ležák), and wheat beers (pšeničné pivo).

Czech Beer Culture and Traditions:

Beer is deeply ingrained in Czech culture and is often considered a staple of daily life and social gatherings. Pubs and beer halls are important meeting places where friends and families come together to enjoy good food, lively conversations, and of course, excellent beer.

Pubs and Beer Halls:

Prague is home to numerous traditional pubs and beer halls where you can enjoy Czech beers in an authentic setting. Some well-known establishments include U Fleků, U Zlatého Tygra, and Lokál. These venues often have a cozy and rustic ambiance, serving a selection of local beers on tap and hearty Czech cuisine.

Beer Gardens:

During the warmer months, Prague's beer gardens come alive, offering a relaxing outdoor setting to enjoy a cold beer and soak in the atmosphere. The Letná Beer Garden and Riegrovy Sady Beer Garden are popular choices.

Craft Beer Scene:

In recent years, Prague has witnessed a growing craft beer movement, with new microbreweries and craft beer bars emerging. These establishments offer a diverse range of beer styles, often experimenting with unique flavors and ingredients. Vinohradský Pivovar, Kocour Brewery, and Pivovarský Dům are some of the local craft breweries to explore.

Beer Tours and Tastings:

Embark on beer tours and tastings to learn about the brewing process, the history of Czech beer, and how to properly appreciate different beer styles. Many beer tours include visits to historic breweries, behind-the-scenes insights, and of course, plenty of beer sampling.

Beer Festivals:

Prague hosts beer festivals throughout the year, such as the Czech Beer Festival, which showcases a wide array of Czech beers from various breweries.

Folklore and Traditional Czech Festivals

Folklore and traditional festivals are an integral part of Czech culture, offering insights into the country's rich history, customs, and heritage. Participating in these festivals allows you to connect with the local community and experience the authentic spirit of Czech traditions. Here are some notable folklore and traditional Czech festivals you might want to explore:

Masopust (Carnival):

Masopust is a pre-Lenten carnival celebrated with colorful parades, masks, costumes, and traditional music. It is a lively and festive time when people indulge in food, drink, and merrymaking before the Lenten period.

Easter Monday Traditions:

On Easter Monday, Czech people partake in the tradition of "pomlázka." Men and boys visit homes, lightly playfully whipping women and girls with braided willow sticks decorated with ribbons, symbolizing health and fertility.

Majáles:

Majáles is a spring festival celebrated by students, featuring parades, live music, dancing, and other festivities. It's a youthful and energetic celebration of the arrival of spring.

International Folklore Festival:

Held in Strážnice, this festival showcases traditional folk music, dance, crafts, and customs from various regions of the Czech Republic and around the world.

Khamoro World Roma Festival:

Celebrates Roma culture through music, dance, theater, and traditional crafts. It offers a unique opportunity to experience the vibrant Roma community's heritage.

Wallachian Open-Air Museum Festivals:

The Wallachian Open-Air Museum hosts various festivals throughout the year, focusing on traditional crafts, music, and customs of the Wallachian region.

Svatý Václav (St. Wenceslas) Day:

Celebrated on September 28th, this holiday honors the patron saint of the Czech lands, St. Wenceslas. It includes processions, religious services, and cultural events.

Pálení čarodějnic (Witches' Night):

Celebrated on April 30th, this holiday involves bonfires, dancing, and burning effigies of witches to symbolize the transition from winter to spring.

Vinobraní (Wine Harvest Festival):

Celebrated in vineyard regions across the country, this festival marks the grape harvest with wine tastings, traditional music, and cultural activities.

Betlém (Nativity Scenes Exhibition):

During the Christmas season, Prague hosts an exhibition of intricately crafted nativity scenes from around the world, showcasing the artistry and devotion of Czech and international artists.

CHARMING STREETS

Prague is renowned for its enchanting streets that showcase a blend of architectural styles, historical charm, and vibrant atmosphere. Here are some of the most charming streets in Prague that you won't want to miss:

Charles Bridge (Karlův Most)

Charles Bridge, known as "Karlův Most" in Czech, is one of the most iconic and picturesque landmarks in Prague. This historic bridge is not only an architectural marvel but also a symbol of the city's rich history and artistic heritage. Here's what you can experience and learn about Charles Bridge:

Historic Significance:

Charles Bridge is a stone Gothic bridge that spans the Vltava River and connects the Old Town (Staré Město) with the Lesser Quarter (Malá Strana) of Prague. It was commissioned by Emperor Charles IV and construction began in 1357.

Unique Architecture:

The bridge features 16 arches and is adorned with 30 statues of saints, most of which were added during the 17th and 18th centuries. These statues create a captivating visual display against the backdrop of the river and city.

Spectacular Views:

Walking across Charles Bridge offers stunning panoramic views of Prague's skyline, including the Prague Castle, St. Vitus Cathedral, and the Old Town Bridge Tower. The views are particularly enchanting during sunrise and sunset.

Street Performers and Artists:

The bridge is often populated with street performers, musicians, and artists, creating a lively and vibrant atmosphere. It's a great place to enjoy live music and witness local talent.

Historical Monuments:

Along the bridge, you'll find the Old Town Bridge Tower and the Lesser Quarter Bridge Tower, both of which are impressive Gothic gateways that once controlled access to the bridge.

Legends and Stories:

Charles Bridge is steeped in legends and stories. One of the most famous legends is that Emperor Charles IV laid the first stone of the bridge during an astrologically auspicious moment, marking the start of a prosperous era for the city.

Nighttime Ambiance:

The bridge takes on a magical ambiance at night when it is beautifully illuminated, creating a romantic and enchanting atmosphere.

Souvenir Stalls:

Along the bridge, you'll find a line of stalls selling souvenirs, artwork, and local crafts. It's a great place to shop for unique gifts and mementos.

Symbol of Prague:

Charles Bridge is not just a means of crossing the river; it is an integral part of Prague's identity and a symbol of its enduring history and culture.

Preservation and Protection:

Due to its historical significance, the foot traffic on the bridge is regulated to preserve its structural integrity. The bridge has undergone several restorations over the centuries to maintain its beauty and ensure its longevity.

Nerudova Street (Nerudova ulice)

Nerudova Street (Nerudova ulice) is a historic and charming cobblestone street located in the Lesser Quarter (Malá Strana) of Prague. Named after the Czech writer Jan Neruda, the street is renowned for its well-preserved architecture, colorful facades, and intriguing atmosphere. Here's what you can experience and explore along Nerudova Street:

Architectural Beauty:

Nerudova Street is lined with a remarkable collection of historic buildings, many of which showcase a mix of architectural styles, including Renaissance, Baroque, and Rococo. The facades are adorned with decorative elements, frescoes, and ornate details.

House Signs:

Each building on Nerudova Street boasts its own unique house sign, often representing the former occupants' professions, symbols, or family crests. These signs offer insight into the history of the street and its inhabitants.

Cobblestone Pathway:

The street's cobblestone pavement adds to its timeless charm and creates a nostalgic atmosphere reminiscent of Prague's past.

Prague Castle Connection:

Nerudova Street is a direct path leading from the Lesser Quarter to Prague Castle. Walking along this street allows you to embark on a historic journey and experience the transition from the city's lower quarters to its elevated castle complex.

Curved and Steep Gradient:

The street's unique curved design and steep gradient provide a sense of exploration and intrigue. As you ascend, you'll encounter charming nooks, alleyways, and hidden corners.

Architectural Details:

Be sure to admire the intricate architectural details, such as wrought-iron balconies, sculpted doorways, and ornate windows, that make each building a work of art.

Neruda's House:

Jan Neruda, the writer after whom the street is named, lived at No. 47 Nerudova Street. His former residence is now a museum dedicated to his life and work.

Curiosities and Legends:

Nerudova Street is rich in legends and stories. For instance, House No. 12, known as "The Two Suns," is said to be haunted. The Loreto House (No. 43) holds a replica of the Santa Casa from Italy.

Shops and Cafes:

Along the street, you'll find an array of boutique shops, art galleries, cafes, and charming eateries. It's a delightful place to explore and enjoy a leisurely stroll.

Views and Atmosphere:

As you ascend Nerudova Street, you'll be treated to glimpses of Prague Castle and panoramic views of the Lesser Quarter. The street's timeless ambiance evokes a sense of stepping back in time.

Golden Lane (Zlatá ulička)

Golden Lane (Zlatá ulička) is a charming and historic lane located within the Prague Castle complex in the Lesser Quarter (Malá Strana) of Prague. This narrow alley is famous for its tiny, colorful houses that once housed castle craftsmen, servants, and alchemists. Here's what you can experience and discover along Golden Lane:

Historic Houses:

The lane is lined with quaint and picturesque houses, each uniquely numbered and named. These houses date back to the late 16th century and early 17th century.

Tiny Structures:

The houses are notably small, with low ceilings and narrow doorways, providing a glimpse into the everyday life of the people who once inhabited them.

Craftsmen and Alchemists:

The houses on Golden Lane were primarily occupied by castle craftsmen, such as goldsmiths and artisans, as well as alchemists who were believed to be working on turning base metals into gold.

Franz Kafka House:

House No. 22 is famous for its association with the renowned writer Franz Kafka. Although Kafka never lived there, it is said that his sister Ottla did reside in this house.

Museum and Exhibitions:

Some of the houses on Golden Lane have been turned into small museums and exhibitions. Visitors can explore these spaces to learn more about the history and life of the people who lived there.

Decorative Facades:

The houses' colorful facades, ornate details, and unique architectural elements make Golden Lane a visually captivating place to explore.

Souvenir Shops:

Some of the houses now serve as souvenir shops, offering a variety of traditional Czech crafts, gifts, and trinkets.

Atmosphere and Ambiance:

Walking along Golden Lane feels like stepping back in time. The narrow alley, historic houses, and cobblestone pavement create a charming and nostalgic atmosphere.

Views of Prague Castle:

As you walk along the lane, you'll enjoy glimpses of Prague Castle's walls, towers, and courtyards, providing a unique perspective of this historic complex.

Timeless Beauty:

Golden Lane's timeless beauty and historical significance make it a popular destination for tourists seeking to experience Prague's rich cultural heritage.

Celetná Street

Celetná Street is a historic and vibrant thoroughfare located in the heart of Prague's Old Town (Staré Město). This bustling street is renowned for its rich history, architectural beauty, and its role as a major commercial and cultural artery in the city. Here's what you can experience and explore along Celetná Street:

Architectural Marvels:

Celetná Street is lined with a stunning array of historical buildings that showcase various architectural styles, including Gothic, Baroque, Renaissance, and Art Nouveau. The facades are adorned with intricate details, decorative elements, and sculpted reliefs.

Old Town Square Connection:

Celetná Street leads directly from the Powder Tower (Prašná brána) to the Old Town Square (Staroměstské náměstí), making it a natural pathway for visitors exploring Prague's iconic landmarks.

Historic Landmarks:

Along the street, you'll encounter several notable landmarks, including the Powder Tower, which once served as a ceremonial entrance to the city, and the House at the Golden Well (Dům U Zlaté Studně), a well-preserved Renaissance building.

Cultural Attractions:

Celetná Street is home to various cultural attractions, such as theaters, galleries, and museums. One of the highlights is the

Museum of Czech Cubism, which showcases the unique artistic movement that emerged in the early 20th century.

Shopping and Dining:

The street features a mix of shops, boutiques, cafes, and restaurants, making it a lively place to shop for souvenirs, fashion, and local products, as well as to indulge in Czech cuisine.

Atmospheric Ambiance:

The street's cobblestone pavement, charming architecture, and bustling atmosphere create an authentic and inviting ambiance that invites exploration.

Historical Context:

Celetná Street has a history dating back to medieval times when it was a major route for trade and commerce. Walking along this street allows you to connect with Prague's past and imagine the bustling activities that once took place here.

Traditional Crafts and Artwork:

Throughout the street, you'll find various workshops and galleries showcasing traditional Czech crafts, such as glassware, jewelry, and artwork.

Festive Events:

Celetná Street often hosts seasonal and cultural events, such as Christmas markets, outdoor concerts, and festivals, adding to its dynamic and vibrant character.

Urban Exploration:

Exploring Celetná Street offers a unique opportunity to immerse yourself in the heart of Prague's historic core and experience the city's blend of past and present.

Na Příkopě Street

Na Příkopě Street is one of Prague's most prominent and bustling thoroughfares, located in the heart of the city's New Town (Nové Město). This vibrant street is renowned for its shopping, historic architecture, and lively atmosphere. Here's what you can experience and explore along Na Příkopě Street:

Shopping Paradise:

Na Příkopě Street is a premier shopping destination in Prague, featuring an array of international and local boutiques, department stores, luxury brands, and fashion outlets.

Architectural Elegance:

The street is lined with elegant buildings that showcase a mix of architectural styles, including Art Nouveau, Neo-

Renaissance, and modern designs. Many of these buildings are adorned with decorative facades and ornate details.

Shopping Centers:

The street is home to several shopping centers, including the prestigious Palladium Shopping Center, which offers a wide range of shops, dining options, and entertainment facilities.

Historical Landmarks:

As you stroll along Na Příkopě Street, you'll pass by important landmarks such as the Church of Our Lady of the Snows (Kostel Panny Marie Sněžné), a stunning Gothic and Baroque church.

Luxury and High-End Shopping:

Na Příkopě is known for its selection of high-end and luxury brands, making it a popular destination for upscale shopping and designer goods.

Cafes and Restaurants:

The street is dotted with cafes, restaurants, and eateries where you can take a break, enjoy a meal, or savor a cup of coffee while watching the bustling city life.

Street Performers and Entertainment:

The lively atmosphere of Na Příkopě often attracts street performers, musicians, and artists, adding a touch of entertainment to your walk.

Historical Context:

Na Příkopě Street has a historical legacy as one of Prague's oldest and most important thoroughfares, initially serving as a medieval moat and later becoming a center of trade and commerce.

Christmas Markets and Festive Events:

During the holiday season, Na Příkopě Street hosts charming Christmas markets and festive events, creating a magical atmosphere.

Urban Experience:

Walking along Na Příkopě Street offers an urban experience that captures the energy, style, and modernity of Prague's New Town, while also connecting you to the city's historical roots.

Liliova Street

Liliova Street is a charming and historic thoroughfare located in the heart of Prague's Old Town (Staré Město). This picturesque street is known for its cobblestone pavement, quaint buildings, and its role as a pathway connecting several significant landmarks. Here's what you can experience and explore along Liliova Street:

Cobblestone Ambiance:

The street's cobblestone pavement and narrow passageway create a charming and romantic atmosphere that harks back to Prague's medieval past.

Central Location:

Liliova Street is centrally located, making it a natural route for visitors exploring the city's historic core. It connects to other famous streets and squares, such as Charles Bridge, Old Town Square, and the Jewish Quarter.

Architectural Details:

The street is adorned with a mix of historical buildings that showcase various architectural styles, including Gothic, Renaissance, and Baroque. Many of the facades feature decorative elements, sculptures, and intricate doorways.

Unique Boutiques and Shops:

Liliova Street offers a selection of boutiques, shops, and galleries where you can find a variety of goods, from souvenirs and local crafts to fashion and accessories.

Cafes and Eateries:

The street is home to cozy cafes and traditional Czech eateries where you can enjoy a meal, indulge in Czech cuisine, or simply take a break and people-watch.

Pathway to Charles Bridge:

Liliova Street is one of the charming routes that leads you to the iconic Charles Bridge, offering a pleasant walk through the Old Town's historic surroundings.

Nearby Landmarks:

While walking along Liliova Street, you'll pass by significant landmarks, such as St. Clement's Cathedral (Kostel sv. Klimenta), a beautiful Baroque church known for its stunning interior.

History and Culture:

The street holds a sense of history and culture, reflecting the essence of Prague's past and its enduring connection to the present.

Nighttime Atmosphere:

Liliova Street takes on a magical quality at night when the buildings are beautifully illuminated, creating a romantic and enchanting ambiance.

Prague's Old World Charm:

Exploring Liliova Street allows you to experience the Old World charm that defines Prague, offering a glimpse into the city's historic character and timeless beauty.

Parizska Street

Parizska Street, also known as "Paris Street," is one of Prague's most prestigious and fashionable boulevards, located in the historic center of the city. This elegant street is renowned for its luxury boutiques, upscale shops, and grand architecture, creating a captivating atmosphere that reflects both Prague's history and modern cosmopolitan flair. Here's what you can experience and discover along Parizska Street:

Luxury Shopping Destination:

Parizska Street is a haven for luxury shopping, featuring an impressive array of high-end designer boutiques, international fashion brands, and fine jewelry stores.

Architectural Beauty:

The street is lined with exquisite buildings that showcase an array of architectural styles, including Art Nouveau, Neo-Renaissance, and Neo-Baroque. The facades are often adorned with intricate details, sculptures, and decorative elements.

Fashion and Accessories:

Parizska Street is a paradise for fashion enthusiasts, offering a wide range of clothing, accessories, footwear, and luxury goods from renowned designers.

Upscale Dining and Cafes:

The boulevard is dotted with chic cafes, elegant restaurants, and stylish eateries where you can indulge in gourmet cuisine and enjoy a sophisticated dining experience.

International Brands:

Many of the world's most prestigious brands have a presence on Parizska Street, making it a destination for those seeking the finest in fashion and luxury.

Art and Culture:

Beyond shopping, the street hosts art galleries, cultural events, and occasional exhibitions, adding a touch of cultural richness to the area.

Historical Context:

The street's name, "Parizska," is a nod to Paris, reflecting the avenue's aspiration to emulate the elegance and sophistication of the French capital.

Architectural Details:

Be sure to admire the exquisite architectural details of the buildings, including ornate balconies, decorative motifs, and elegant entrances.

Seasonal Decorations:

Parizska Street is often beautifully decorated during the holiday season, creating a festive and enchanting ambiance that adds to the street's allure.

People-Watching and Glamour:

Parizska Street offers the opportunity for people-watching and soaking up the glamorous atmosphere. It's a place to see and be seen, especially among those who appreciate fine living and fashion.

Železná Street

Železná Street, located in the historic center of Prague's Old Town (Staré Město), is a charming and picturesque street known for its cobblestone pavement, historic architecture, and vibrant atmosphere. This pedestrian-friendly street offers a mix of shops, cafes, and historic sites, making it a delightful destination for both locals and visitors. Here's what you can experience and explore along Železná Street:

Historic Ambiance:

Železná Street exudes a sense of history and authenticity, with its well-preserved buildings and cobblestone surface that transport you back in time.

Architectural Details:

The street is lined with buildings that showcase various architectural styles, including Gothic, Renaissance, and Baroque. Admire the decorative facades, ornate windows, and unique doorways.

Central Location:

Železná Street is centrally located, providing easy access to many of Prague's iconic attractions, including the Old Town Square, Charles Bridge, and the Jewish Quarter.

Shops and Boutiques:

The street features a mix of shops, boutiques, and galleries where you can find a variety of goods, including fashion, jewelry, souvenirs, and local crafts.

Cafes and Restaurants:

Enjoy a leisurely meal or a cup of coffee at the charming cafes and eateries along Železná Street. It's a great place to relax and people-watch.

Nightlife and Entertainment:

As the day transitions into evening, Železná Street comes alive with a vibrant nightlife scene. Discover bars, pubs, and live music venues where you can unwind and enjoy the local atmosphere.

Jewish Sites:

Near the end of Železná Street, you'll find the Jewish Quarter (Josefov) with its historic synagogues, cemetery, and cultural landmarks.

Street Performers and Events:

The street often hosts street performers, musicians, and events, adding to its lively and dynamic character.

Historical Context:

Železná Street has a history dating back to medieval times and has witnessed the evolution of Prague's Old Town throughout the centuries.

Authentic Experience:

Walking along Železná Street offers an authentic Prague experience, allowing you to immerse yourself in the city's charming architecture, local culture, and vibrant street life.

Malá Strana Streets

Malá Strana, or the Lesser Quarter, is a picturesque neighborhood in Prague that boasts a maze of charming streets and alleys. This historic area is located just below Prague Castle and is known for its romantic atmosphere, stunning architecture, and cultural treasures. Here's what you can experience as you wander through the enchanting streets of Malá Strana:

Cobblestone Pathways:

The streets of Malá Strana are often adorned with cobblestones, adding to the area's timeless and romantic ambiance.

Baroque Architecture:

The neighborhood is renowned for its well-preserved Baroque buildings, many of which feature ornate facades, sculpted reliefs, and grand entrances.

Colorful Houses:

The facades of the houses are often painted in a variety of colors, creating a picturesque and vibrant scene as you explore the streets.

Peaceful Alleys:

Malá Strana's narrow alleys and side streets provide a peaceful escape from the bustling city, inviting you to take leisurely walks and discover hidden gems.

Art Galleries and Studios:

The neighborhood is home to numerous art galleries, studios, and workshops, where you can discover local artists and their creations.

Historical Landmarks:

As you wander through Malá Strana, you'll encounter significant landmarks, including St. Nicholas Church, Wallenstein Palace, and the Infant Jesus of Prague.

Cafes and Restaurants:

Charming cafes, restaurants, and eateries are nestled throughout Malá Strana, offering a variety of dining options and places to rest.

Vrtbovská Garden:

This beautiful Baroque garden is a hidden gem within Malá Strana, offering breathtaking views of the city and a serene oasis.

Lennon Wall:

The famous Lennon Wall is a colorful tribute to John Lennon and a symbol of peace and free expression. It's a unique artistic landmark in the heart of Malá Strana.

Charles Bridge Connection:

Malá Strana is connected to the Old Town by the iconic Charles Bridge, offering a scenic route for crossing the Vltava River.

NATURE GUIDE

While Prague is known for its historical and cultural attractions, the city also offers opportunities to connect with nature. Here are some ways to experience nature in and around Prague:

Vltava River

The Vltava River is a central and iconic feature of Prague, flowing through the heart of the city and playing a significant role in its history, culture, and daily life. Here's a closer look at the Vltava River and the experiences it offers:

Scenic Views and Walks:

The riverbanks of the Vltava offer some of the most picturesque views of Prague's landmarks, including Prague Castle, Charles Bridge, and the National Theatre. Strolling along the river's embankments, such as Naplavka, provides a relaxing and charming way to experience the city's architecture and atmosphere.

Charles Bridge:

The iconic Charles Bridge spans the Vltava River and is one of Prague's most famous landmarks. It's a favorite spot for both tourists and locals, offering stunning views of the river and the city.

Boat Cruises:

Boat cruises on the Vltava River allow you to see Prague from a different perspective. Choose from a variety of options, including sightseeing cruises, dinner cruises, and even jazz or live music cruises.

Kayaking and Canoeing:

For those seeking a more active experience, kayaking and canoeing on the Vltava provide a unique way to explore the city's landmarks and bridges while enjoying the tranquility of the water.

Dancing House:

The modern and unconventional Dancing House, designed by architects Frank Gehry and Vlado Milunić, stands out along the river's bank and adds an interesting contrast to Prague's historical architecture.

Vltava Embankments and Events:

The Vltava's embankments, such as Smetanovo nábřeží and Rašínovo nábřeží, are vibrant gathering spots with restaurants, cafés, and occasional cultural events.

Photography Opportunities:

Photographers will find numerous vantage points along the river to capture breathtaking shots of Prague's skyline and reflections on the water.

Relaxation and Reflection:

The Vltava River provides a serene backdrop for moments of relaxation, whether you're sitting on a bench, enjoying a cup of coffee, or simply watching the river flow by.

Prague Zoo

The Prague Zoo is a popular and highly regarded attraction that offers visitors the chance to explore a diverse range of animal species from around the world in a beautiful and natural setting. Here's what you can expect to experience at the Prague Zoo:

Diverse Animal Exhibits:

The Prague Zoo is home to over 650 animal species, including mammals, birds, reptiles, amphibians, and fish. Each exhibit is designed to mimic the animals' natural habitats as closely as possible.

Ecosystems and Habitats:

The zoo is divided into thematic areas that represent different ecosystems and regions, such as the African Savannah, Indonesian Jungle, and Gorilla Pavilion.

Conservation Efforts:

The Prague Zoo places a strong emphasis on conservation and participates in various international breeding and reintroduction programs to help endangered species.

Elephant Valley:

One of the highlights is the Elephant Valley, a spacious and modern enclosure for the zoo's elephants, designed to provide them with a more natural and comfortable environment.

Children's Area:

The Children's Zoo is a favorite among young visitors, offering interactive experiences, petting areas, and a chance to get up close with domestic animals.

Primate Pavilions:

The zoo features several primate pavilions where you can observe various species of monkeys and apes in environments that closely resemble their native habitats.

Conservation Projects and Education:

The zoo is committed to educating visitors about the importance of conservation and biodiversity through informative exhibits, interactive displays, and educational programs.

Events and Workshops:

The zoo organizes events, workshops, and activities for visitors of all ages, including guided tours, animal feeding demonstrations, and seasonal celebrations.

Botanical Gardens:

In addition to its animal exhibits, the Prague Zoo boasts beautiful botanical gardens with a wide variety of plant species from around the world.

Scenic Views and Relaxation:

The zoo's location on the banks of the Vltava River offers stunning views of the city's skyline. Visitors can also relax in various green spaces and picnic areas.

Žižkov Television Tower

The Žižkov Television Tower is one of Prague's most distinctive and unique landmarks, known for its futuristic design and the various artistic installations that adorn its exterior. Here's what you can expect to experience at the Žižkov Television Tower:

Architectural Icon:

The tower stands as a striking contrast to Prague's historical architecture, with its unconventional and avant-garde design. It was completed in the 1980s during the communist era.

Observation Deck:

The tower's observation deck, located at a height of around 93 meters (305 feet), offers panoramic views of Prague and its surroundings. On a clear day, you can see landmarks such as Prague Castle, Charles Bridge, and Old Town Square.

Sculptural Installations:

The tower's exterior is adorned with sculptures by Czech artist David Černý, known for his thought-provoking and often humorous artworks. One notable installation is the crawling babies, which adds an intriguing and unconventional touch to the tower's appearance.

Restaurant and Bar:

The tower features a restaurant and bar where you can enjoy a meal or a drink while taking in the views. The rotating restaurant slowly rotates 360 degrees, allowing you to enjoy different perspectives of the city.

Zizkov Neighborhood:

The tower is located in the Žižkov neighborhood, known for its vibrant and bohemian atmosphere. Exploring the area around the tower gives you a chance to experience a different side of Prague, with its local cafes, art galleries, and street art.

Cultural Events:

The Žižkov Television Tower occasionally hosts cultural events, exhibitions, and performances, adding to its role as a cultural hub in the city.

Photography:

The tower's unique design and artistic installations make it a popular subject for photographers looking to capture Prague from a different angle.

Petřín Hill and Gardens

Petřín Hill and Gardens are a delightful natural oasis located in the heart of Prague, offering a peaceful retreat from the bustling city streets. Here's a closer look at what you can experience at Petřín Hill and Gardens:

Petřín Lookout Tower:

Resembling a miniature Eiffel Tower, the Petřín Lookout Tower offers panoramic views of Prague from its observation deck. You can either climb the 299 steps or take the funicular railway to reach the top.

Walking Paths and Gardens:

Petřín Hill is crisscrossed by walking paths and trails that lead through beautifully landscaped gardens, wooded areas, and open spaces.

The gardens are meticulously maintained and provide a serene environment for relaxation, picnics, or leisurely strolls.

Rose Garden:

The Rose Garden is a highlight of Petřín Gardens, especially during the blooming season (typically from May to September). It features a colorful array of roses in various shapes and colors.

Mirror Maze:

Inspired by the gardens of Versailles, the Mirror Maze is a fun attraction where you can get lost in a maze of mirrors and illusions.

Hunger Wall:

The Hunger Wall, also known as the Wall of Prague, was built in the 14th century to provide employment for the poor during times of famine. It stretches along the hillside and offers historic insights.

Nebozízek Garden Restaurant:

Enjoy a meal or a refreshing drink at the Nebozízek Garden Restaurant while taking in scenic views of the city.

Miniature Eiffel Tower:

Apart from the lookout tower, you'll also find a smaller replica of the Eiffel Tower at Petřín Hill, adding a touch of Parisian charm to the landscape.

Petřín Funicular:

The funicular railway is a convenient way to reach the top of Petřín Hill, offering a short and scenic ride that connects the Lesser Town to the hill's summit.

Exercise and Recreation:

The hill's paths are popular among locals and visitors for jogging, hiking, and exercising. The peaceful surroundings make it a great place to clear your mind and connect with nature.

Letná Park

Letná Park is a beautiful and spacious urban park located on a hill overlooking the Vltava River and the city of Prague. It's a favorite destination for both locals and visitors who seek a peaceful escape, stunning views, and recreational opportunities. Here's what you can experience at Letná Park:

Panoramic Views:

Letná Park offers some of the most breathtaking panoramic views of Prague's skyline, the Vltava River, and its historic bridges. It's a popular spot for capturing stunning photographs of the city.

Metronome Sculpture:

The iconic Metronome sculpture is a prominent feature of the park, located on the site where a massive statue of Joseph Stalin once stood. The Metronome has become a symbol of the city's transformation and offers a unique backdrop for events and gatherings.

Walking and Jogging:

The park is crisscrossed with walking and jogging paths that wind through lush greenery, providing a peaceful environment for outdoor exercise.

Beer Garden and Refreshments:

Letná Park features a popular beer garden where you can enjoy a cold Czech beer, relax with friends, and savor local cuisine while taking in the panoramic views.

Picnics and Relaxation:

The park's open spaces and benches are perfect for picnics, reading, or simply unwinding amidst nature.

Outdoor Art Installations:

Letná Park occasionally hosts outdoor art installations, sculptures, and cultural events that add to its vibrant atmosphere.

Sports and Recreation:

The park has areas designated for sports and recreational activities, including basketball courts, a skatepark, and a playground for children.

Events and Festivals:

Letná Park is a popular venue for various events, including concerts, festivals, and public gatherings. It has hosted music festivals, cultural exhibitions, and more.

Relaxing Strolls:

The park's serene ambiance, shaded pathways, and well-maintained gardens make it an inviting place for leisurely strolls and moments of reflection.

Stromovka Park

Stromovka Park is one of Prague's largest and most beloved urban parks, offering a spacious and tranquil oasis where visitors can enjoy nature, engage in recreational activities, and unwind. Here's what you can experience at Stromovka Park:

Vast Green Spaces:

Stromovka Park features expansive lawns, meadows, and tree-lined avenues that provide ample space for picnics, outdoor games, and relaxation.

Walking and Jogging Paths:

The park offers well-maintained walking and jogging paths that wind through its lush landscapes, providing a serene environment for exercise and leisurely strolls.

Lakes and Ponds:

The park is home to several lakes and ponds, including Velká strouha and Malá strouha. These water bodies contribute to the park's tranquil ambiance and are often visited by ducks and other waterfowl.

Rowing and Boating:

Velká strouha lake allows for rowing and paddle boating during the warmer months, providing a unique way to experience the park from the water.

Picnic Areas:

Numerous designated picnic areas with benches and tables are scattered throughout the park, providing ideal spots to enjoy a meal surrounded by nature.

Playgrounds and Sports Facilities:

Stromovka Park features playgrounds for children, as well as sports facilities such as tennis courts, volleyball courts, and a skate park.

Historical Monuments:

The park is dotted with historical monuments, including the Chateau of Prague Exhibition Grounds, the Governor's Summer Palace, and various statues and sculptures.

Cultural Events and Festivals:

Stromovka hosts cultural events, concerts, and festivals throughout the year. It's a popular venue for outdoor performances and gatherings.

Relaxation and Birdwatching:

The park's peaceful environment makes it an ideal place for relaxation, meditation, or birdwatching. You may spot various bird species, including swans and herons.

Dog-Friendly Space:

Stromovka is a dog-friendly park, allowing visitors to enjoy the outdoors with their furry companions. There's even a designated off-leash area for dogs.

Vyšehrad Park

Vyšehrad Park is a historic and picturesque green space located atop a rocky hill overlooking the Vltava River in Prague. This park is not only a peaceful oasis but also holds significant cultural and historical importance. Here's what you can experience at Vyšehrad Park:

Vyšehrad Fortress:

The park is dominated by the Vyšehrad Fortress, a historic stronghold that dates back to the 10th century. The fortress includes remnants of the original fortifications, such as the Gothic entrance gate and the iconic Basilica of St. Peter and St. Paul.

Panoramic Views:

Vyšehrad Park offers breathtaking panoramic views of Prague, including Prague Castle, Charles Bridge, and the city skyline. It's a popular spot for photographers and anyone looking to admire the city from a different perspective.

Historic Cemetery:

The Vyšehrad Cemetery is the final resting place of many notable Czech figures, including artists, writers, composers, and politicians. It's a serene and reflective place to explore.

Rotunda of St. Martin:

This Romanesque rotunda is one of the oldest preserved buildings in Prague and is located within Vyšehrad Park. It's a testament to the park's rich history.

Walking Paths and Gardens:

The park features pleasant walking paths that wind through well-maintained gardens, offering a peaceful environment for leisurely strolls and relaxation.

Monument to the Victims of Communism:

A powerful monument dedicated to the victims of the Communist regime in Czechoslovakia is located within the park. It serves as a reminder of the country's tumultuous history.

Cultural Events:

Vyšehrad Park hosts various cultural events, including open-air concerts, performances, and festivals, especially during the summer months.

Legendary Legends:

Vyšehrad is associated with numerous legends and myths from Czech folklore, adding to the park's mystique and allure.

Sculptures and Statues:

Throughout the park, you'll come across sculptures and statues that contribute to the artistic and historical ambiance.

Relaxation and Nature:

Whether you're seeking a quiet place to relax, enjoy a peaceful walk, or learn about Czech history and culture, Vyšehrad Park offers a serene and historically rich setting.

Kampa Park

Kampa Park is a charming and picturesque island park situated in the heart of Prague, bordered by the Vltava River and the Čertovka canal. Known for its serene atmosphere, beautiful views, and artistic ambiance, Kampa Park offers a unique and delightful experience. Here's what you can expect to experience at Kampa Park:

Riverside Location:

Kampa Park's location along the Vltava River and Čertovka canal provides stunning views of the water, historic bridges, and Prague Castle in the distance.

Artistic Vibes:

Kampa has a creative and artistic atmosphere, with galleries, sculptures, and installations scattered throughout the park. It's a favorite spot for art lovers and those seeking a unique cultural experience.

Playground and Petting Zoo:

Kampa Park is family-friendly, offering a playground for children to enjoy and a small petting zoo where kids can interact with animals.

Cobblestone Streets:

The park's cobblestone streets and charming pathways create a quaint and historic atmosphere that complements the surrounding architecture.

Picnicking and Relaxation:

Kampa Park is a perfect place for picnics, with grassy areas and benches where you can relax and enjoy a meal or a book.

Charles Bridge Views:

The park's location near the Charles Bridge allows you to enjoy picturesque views of this iconic landmark from different angles.

Unique Cafés and Restaurants:

Kampa Park is home to several cozy cafés and restaurants where you can enjoy a meal or a drink while taking in the park's ambiance.

Outdoor Events:

Kampa Park hosts various outdoor events, performances, and cultural activities, especially during the warmer months.

Lennon Wall:

One of Kampa Park's most iconic features is the Lennon Wall, a colorful mural dedicated to John Lennon and inspired by his message of peace and love. Visitors are welcome to add their own messages and artwork to the wall.

Romantic Atmosphere:

With its tranquil waterways, art installations, and historic surroundings, Kampa Park is a popular spot for couples and those seeking a romantic escape.

Royal Garden at Prague Castle

The Royal Garden at Prague Castle is a meticulously landscaped and historically significant garden that surrounds the iconic Prague Castle. With its elegant design, diverse flora, and historical monuments, the Royal Garden offers visitors a serene retreat within the heart of the city. Here's what you can experience at the Royal Garden:

Renaissance Design:

The Royal Garden is designed in the Renaissance style, featuring geometric patterns, terraced levels, and symmetrical layouts that reflect the artistic trends of the 16th century.

Summer Palace and Ball Game Hall:

The Summer Palace is an exquisite example of Renaissance architecture, and it serves as the centerpiece of the garden. The Ball Game Hall is a unique building where traditional games were once played.

Singing Fountain:

The Singing Fountain is an ornate Baroque fountain that adds a touch of elegance to the garden. It's a peaceful spot to relax and admire the surrounding beauty.

Scenic Views:

The garden offers scenic views of Prague Castle, its towers, and the surrounding city. It's a great place to capture photographs and enjoy the architectural splendor.

Ornamental Flower Beds:

The garden is adorned with colorful and meticulously maintained flower beds, showcasing a variety of seasonal blooms that add to the visual appeal.

Labyrinth and Maze:

The Royal Garden features a labyrinth and a hedge maze, offering a playful and engaging experience for visitors of all ages.

Orangery:

The Orangery is a greenhouse that houses delicate plants during the winter months. It's a charming structure that adds to the garden's ambiance.

Herb Garden:

The garden includes a section dedicated to herbs and medicinal plants, reflecting its historical role in providing ingredients for the royal court.

Tranquil Atmosphere:

The Royal Garden offers a tranquil and peaceful atmosphere, making it a perfect place for leisurely walks, quiet contemplation, or escaping the crowds of the city.

Events and Concerts:

The Royal Garden occasionally hosts events, concerts, and cultural activities that add to its vibrant and dynamic character.

Wallenstein Garden

The Wallenstein Garden (Valdštejnská zahrada) is a splendid Baroque garden located in the Lesser Quarter of Prague, adjacent to the Wallenstein Palace. Known for its meticulously designed layout, ornate sculptures, and tranquil ambiance, the Wallenstein Garden is a serene oasis in the heart of the city. Here's what you can experience at the Wallenstein Garden:

Baroque Design:

The Wallenstein Garden showcases a classic Baroque design characterized by symmetrical patterns, geometric shapes, and carefully manicured lawns.

Sala Terrena:

The Sala Terrena is a grand hall located at the entrance of the garden. It features elegant architecture, intricate frescoes, and a stunning view of the central fountain.

Central Fountain:

The central feature of the garden is a large, gushing fountain adorned with statues of mythical figures, animals, and sea creatures. It's a mesmerizing sight and a focal point of the garden.

Wallenstein Palace:

The garden is adjacent to the Wallenstein Palace, a magnificent Baroque palace that once served as the residence of the Wallenstein family. While the palace is not open to the public, you can admire its grand exterior from the garden.

Allegorical Sculptures:

The garden is adorned with numerous statues and sculptures depicting mythological and allegorical figures, adding an artistic and historical dimension to the surroundings.

Labyrinth and Pavilion:

The garden features a labyrinth and a charming pavilion, inviting visitors to explore and find hidden corners within the lush landscape.

Peacocks and Wildlife:

The garden is home to a small population of peacocks that freely roam the grounds, adding a touch of whimsy and natural beauty.

Historic Atmosphere:

Stepping into the Wallenstein Garden feels like entering a different era. The preserved Baroque elements and meticulous landscaping transport visitors back in time.

Relaxation and Contemplation:

The tranquil atmosphere and well-kept lawns make the Wallenstein Garden an ideal place for relaxation, picnics, or moments of quiet contemplation.

Seasonal Beauty:

The garden's beauty changes with the seasons, offering different colors and blooms throughout the year. Spring and summer are particularly enchanting times to visit.

Riegrovy Sady Park

Riegrovy Sady Park is a popular urban park located in the Vinohrady district of Prague. This spacious and vibrant park offers a diverse range of activities, scenic viewpoints, and a lively atmosphere, making it a favorite spot for both locals and visitors. Here's what you can experience at Riegrovy Sady Park:

Expansive Green Space:

Riegrovy Sady is known for its large open lawns, providing ample space for picnics, sunbathing, and various outdoor activities.

Panoramic Views:

The park offers stunning panoramic views of the city center, including Prague Castle, Old Town, and the Vltava River. It's a popular spot to watch the sunset and capture cityscape photographs.

Beer Garden:

The park's beer garden, Riegrovy Sady Beer Garden, is a beloved gathering place. It offers a wide selection of Czech beers on tap, making it a perfect spot to relax and socialize.

Outdoor Screenings and Events:

Riegrovy Sady hosts outdoor screenings of sports events, movies, and cultural performances, creating a lively and festive atmosphere.

Playground and Sports Facilities:

The park features a playground for children and sports facilities for activities such as volleyball, table tennis, and street workout.

Relaxation and Recreation:

Whether you're interested in active pursuits, leisurely walks, or simply enjoying the outdoors, Riegrovy Sady offers a space for relaxation and recreation.

Pet-Friendly Environment:

The park is pet-friendly, allowing visitors to bring their dogs for a walk or playtime.

Seasonal Beauty:

Riegrovy Sady's appearance changes with the seasons, offering colorful blooms in spring, lush greenery in summer, and vibrant foliage in autumn.

Local Vibe:

The park's central location within the Vinohrady neighborhood provides a glimpse into the local lifestyle and a chance to connect with residents.

Community Feel:

Riegrovy Sady often hosts community events, cultural festivals, and gatherings that bring people together and contribute to the park's vibrant atmosphere.

Havlíčkovy Sady Park (Grébovka)

Havlíčkovy Sady Park, often referred to as Grébovka, is a charming and picturesque park located in the Vinohrady district of Prague. Known for its elegant gardens, vineyards, historic pavilions, and tranquil atmosphere, Havlíčkovy Sady offers a unique and delightful experience for visitors. Here's what you can expect to experience at Havlíčkovy Sady Park:

Vineyards:

One of the distinctive features of the park is its vineyards, which produce Czech wines. You can take a leisurely stroll through the vineyards and enjoy the picturesque setting.

Pavilion and Gazebo:

The park is home to the Grébovka Pavilion, a charming Neo-Renaissance building where you can relax and enjoy refreshments. There's also a delightful gazebo in the park that adds to its romantic ambiance.

Rose Garden:

Havlíčkovy Sady is famous for its beautiful Rose Garden, featuring a variety of rose species and vibrant colors. It's a favorite spot for nature enthusiasts and photography enthusiasts.

Relaxation and Picnics:

The park's well-maintained lawns, benches, and shaded areas make it a perfect spot for picnics, relaxation, and enjoying nature.

Splendid Architecture:

In addition to the pavilions, the park is adorned with ornate architectural elements, creating a visually appealing environment.

Scenic Views:

Havlíčkovy Sady offers scenic viewpoints where you can enjoy panoramic vistas of Prague's skyline and historic landmarks.

Statues and Sculptures:

Throughout the park, you'll discover statues and sculptures that contribute to the park's artistic and cultural ambiance.

Romantic Atmosphere:

Havlíčkovy Sady's charming gardens, elegant pavilions, and tranquil setting make it a popular spot for couples seeking a romantic escape.

Photography Opportunities:

The park's natural beauty and architectural details provide ample opportunities for photography, whether you're capturing the lush landscapes or focusing on intricate details.

Events and Festivals:

Havlíčkovy Sady occasionally hosts cultural events, outdoor concerts, and festivals, adding to its lively and dynamic character.

Divoká Šárka Nature Reserve

Divoká Šárka is a stunning and picturesque nature reserve located on thc outskirts of Prague, Czech Republic. It's a popular destination for nature enthusiasts, hikers, and those seeking a refreshing escape from urban life. Here's what you can experience at Divoká Šárka Nature Reserve:

Natural Beauty:

Divoká Šárka is known for its breathtaking natural landscapes, including deep ravines, rugged cliffs, lush forests, and a crystal-clear stream that winds through the area.

Hiking Trails:

The nature reserve offers a network of well-marked hiking trails that cater to various levels of difficulty. These trails provide opportunities to explore the diverse terrain and enjoy panoramic views.

Rock Formations:

The reserve is characterized by unique rock formations and cliffs, which are popular among rock climbers, boulderers, and adventure seekers.

Divoká Šárka Ravine:

The ravine itself is a natural wonder, with its steep slopes, dense vegetation, and the tranquil stream flowing through it. It's an ideal spot for peaceful walks and nature observation.

Natural Swimming Pool (Amerika):

One of the highlights is the natural swimming pool known as "Amerika." This refreshing pool is fed by a spring and is a popular spot for swimming during the summer months.

Wildlife and Flora:

Divoká Šárka is home to a variety of plant and animal species. You may encounter foxes, squirrels, various bird species, and even the elusive European green lizard.

Biking Trails:

The reserve has designated mountain biking trails that allow cyclists to explore the area's diverse landscapes while enjoying an active outdoor experience.

Relaxation and Picnics:

Divoká Šárka provides plenty of peaceful spots for relaxation, picnics, and enjoying the serenity of nature.

Summer Cinema:

During the summer months, an outdoor cinema operates in the reserve, offering a unique movie-watching experience in a natural setting.

Cultural and Historical Significance:

The reserve's name is derived from a legendary Czech warrior maiden, Šárka. It also holds archaeological significance, with evidence of prehistoric settlements.

Franciscan Garden

The Franciscan Garden (Františkánská zahrada) is a peaceful and charming oasis nestled in the heart of Prague's New Town, offering a serene escape from the city's bustling streets. With its well-maintained lawns, colorful flowerbeds, and tranquil atmosphere, the Franciscan Garden provides a pleasant respite for both locals and visitors. Here's what you can experience at the Franciscan Garden:

Tranquil Atmosphere:

The garden's quiet ambiance makes it an ideal place for relaxation, meditation, and taking a break from the urban environment.

Central Location:

The Franciscan Garden is conveniently located near Wenceslas Square, making it easily accessible for a brief getaway.

Well-Maintained Gardens:

The garden features manicured lawns, vibrant flowerbeds, and a variety of plants that contribute to its picturesque beauty.

Fountain and Benches:

A central fountain serves as a focal point of the garden, and benches are scattered throughout, providing comfortable spots to sit and enjoy the surroundings.

Peaceful Pathways:

The garden has well-laid pathways that invite visitors to take leisurely strolls amidst the greenery.

Relaxation and Reading:

The quiet ambiance and comfortable benches make the garden a popular spot for reading and unwinding.

Statues and Sculptures:

The garden is adorned with sculptures and statues that add to its artistic and cultural appeal.

Dog-Friendly Space:

The Franciscan Garden is dog-friendly, allowing visitors to bring their furry companions for a walk and some fresh air.

Seasonal Beauty:

Throughout the year, the garden displays different blooms and foliage, offering changing displays of color and vibrancy.

Photographic Opportunities:

The garden's serene beauty and artistic elements provide opportunities for capturing lovely photographs.

Trojská Zahrada

Trojská zahrada, also known as the Troja Garden, is a beautiful botanical garden located in Prague, Czech Republic. It's situated in the Troja district, which is known for its historic and cultural attractions. Here's a brief overview of Trojská zahrada:

Location:

Trojská zahrada is located in the Troja district of Prague, near the Prague Zoo and the Troja Chateau. Its address is Trojská 800/196, 171 00 Prague 7.

Historical Background:

The garden is situated on the grounds of the Troja Chateau, a Baroque palace that dates back to the 17th century. The chateau and the garden were designed to complement each other, creating a harmonious blend of architecture and nature.

Garden Design:

Trojská zahrada features formal Baroque-style gardens with symmetrically arranged flowerbeds, hedges, and statues. The garden's layout is inspired by French and Italian Renaissance garden designs, characterized by geometric patterns and elaborate landscaping.

Fountains and Sculptures:

The garden is adorned with a variety of sculptures and decorative elements, including fountains, statues, and ornamental vases. These sculptures contribute to the garden's artistic and historical ambiance.

Plant Collections:

Trojská zahrada is home to a diverse collection of plants, including both native and exotic species. The garden features well-maintained flowerbeds, shrubs, and trees, creating a visually stunning landscape throughout the year.

Views of the Vltava River:

From certain vantage points within the garden, visitors can enjoy panoramic views of the Vltava River and the Prague skyline. This makes the garden an ideal place for relaxation and photography.

Events and Exhibitions:

Trojská zahrada occasionally hosts cultural events, exhibitions, and performances, which further enrich the visitor experience. These events can range from art exhibitions to music concerts.

Accessibility:

The garden is accessible by public transportation, and visitors can reach it via tram or bus. The Troja Chateau and the garden are located near the Prague Zoo, making it convenient to explore multiple attractions in the same area.

Opening Hours and Admission:

The garden's opening hours and admission fees may vary depending on the season and any special events. It's recommended to check the official website or contact the Troja Chateau for the most up-to-date information.

Nearby Attractions:

In addition to Trojská zahrada, visitors can explore other attractions in the Troja district, such as the Troja Chateau and the Prague Zoo. The combination of these attractions offers a well-rounded experience of history, nature, and culture.

AMAZING CATHEDRALS

Prague is home to several magnificent cathedrals that showcase stunning architecture, rich history, and intricate artistic details. These cathedrals are not only religious landmarks but also important cultural and historical sites. Here are some of the amazing cathedrals you can visit in Prague:

St. Vitus Cathedral

St. Vitus Cathedral, known as "Katedrála svatého Víta" in Czech, is one of the most magnificent and significant landmarks in Prague. Located within the Prague Castle complex, this Gothic cathedral is not only a religious site but also a symbol of Czech history, culture, and architectural prowess. Here's what you can learn about and experience at St. Vitus Cathedral:

Architectural Marvel:

St. Vitus Cathedral is a masterpiece of Gothic architecture, characterized by its soaring spires, intricate stone carvings, and stunning stained glass windows. The cathedral's construction spanned centuries, resulting in a blend of architectural styles, including Gothic, Renaissance, and Baroque elements.

Stunning Facade:

The exterior facade of St. Vitus Cathedral is adorned with intricate sculptures, reliefs, and decorative details that tell stories from the Bible and Czech history.

St. Wenceslas Chapel:

One of the most revered parts of the cathedral is the St. Wenceslas Chapel, a beautiful space adorned with richly colored frescoes, gilded decorations, and a precious relic of St. Wenceslas, the patron saint of the Czech lands.

Royal Mausoleum:

St. Vitus Cathedral is the final resting place of many Czech monarchs and historical figures. The tombs and chapels within the cathedral complex provide a glimpse into the country's royal history.

Stained Glass Windows:

The cathedral's stained glass windows are breathtaking works of art that illuminate the interior with vibrant colors and intricate designs. The windows depict scenes from the Bible and the lives of saints.

Bell Tower and Views:

Visitors can climb the cathedral's bell tower for panoramic views of Prague and the surrounding areas. The tower offers a unique perspective of the city's skyline and the Prague Castle complex.

Religious Services and Events:

St. Vitus Cathedral continues to serve as a place of worship and hosts religious services, concerts, and cultural events, adding to its vibrant and living history.

Historical Significance:

The cathedral has played a central role in Czech history, hosting important coronations, royal ceremonies, and historical events. Its presence has shaped the cultural and architectural identity of Prague.

Artistic Treasures:

The interior of St. Vitus Cathedral is adorned with intricate sculptures, altars, and artwork that reflect the artistic achievements of different eras.

Spiritual Experience:

Whether you're interested in history, architecture, or spirituality, a visit to St. Vitus Cathedral offers a profound and awe-inspiring experience that connects you to the cultural and religious heritage of Prague and the Czech Republic.

St. Nicholas Church

St. Nicholas Church (Kostel svatého Mikuláše) is a spectacular Baroque masterpiece located in the heart of Prague's Lesser Quarter (Malá Strana). Its grandeur, stunning interior, and impressive dome make it one of the most iconic and recognizable landmarks in the city. Here's what you can learn about and experience at St. Nicholas Church:

Baroque Splendor:

St. Nicholas Church is a prime example of Baroque architecture, characterized by its opulent decorations, elaborate stucco work, and lavish gilded details. The church's interior is a celebration of the Baroque style's exuberance and artistic achievement.

Impressive Dome:

The church's central dome is a striking feature that dominates the interior. The dome is adorned with intricate frescoes depicting scenes from the life of St. Nicholas and other biblical stories.

Altarpieces:

St. Nicholas Church boasts several ornate altarpieces, including the main high altar and side altars. These altars are adorned with intricate sculptures and elaborate design elements.

Stucco Decorations:

The walls and ceilings of the church are adorned with intricate stucco decorations, creating a sense of movement and dynamism throughout the interior.

Pipe Organ:

The church is home to a magnificent pipe organ, considered one of the finest Baroque organs in Europe. The organ's intricate design and exceptional acoustics make it a highlight for music enthusiasts.

Concerts and Events:

St. Nicholas Church is a popular venue for classical music concerts and cultural events. Attending a concert here provides a unique opportunity to experience the church's acoustics and immerse yourself in a musical performance.

Historical Significance:

The church has played a significant role in Czech history and culture, hosting important events and ceremonies over the centuries.

Panoramic Views:

For those willing to climb to the church's tower, panoramic views of the Lesser Quarter and the city's historic center await. The tower offers a breathtaking perspective of Prague's skyline.

Religious Services:

St. Nicholas Church continues to serve as a place of worship, hosting regular religious services and providing a serene space for contemplation.

Artistic Achievement:

Visiting St. Nicholas Church allows you to appreciate the extraordinary artistic talent that went into its creation. From the intricate sculptures to the vibrant frescoes, every corner of the church is a testament to human creativity.

Church of Our Lady before Týn

The Church of Our Lady before Týn (Kostel Matky Boží před Týnem) is a captivating Gothic masterpiece that graces the skyline of Prague's Old Town Square. Its distinctive twin towers and intricate facade make it one of the most recognizable and iconic landmarks in the city. Here's what you can learn about and experience at the Church of Our Lady before Týn:

Architectural Marvel:

The church's twin towers, soaring to impressive heights, are a defining feature of Prague's skyline. The Gothic architecture is characterized by pointed arches, intricate tracery, and ornate decorations.

Unique Facade:

The facade of the Church of Our Lady before Týn is adorned with a wealth of decorative details, sculptures, and reliefs. The entrance is flanked by statues of the Virgin Mary and other religious figures.

Interior Beauty:

The interior of the church boasts a stunning nave with high vaulted ceilings, intricate stone carvings, and beautiful stained glass windows that bathe the space in colorful light.

Jan Hus Connection:

The Church of Our Lady before Týn has historical significance as a place associated with Jan Hus, a Czech religious reformer and martyr. His teachings influenced the Hussite movement in Bohemia.

Religious Services:

The church continues to be an active place of worship, hosting regular religious services and ceremonies. Attending a service here offers a chance to experience its spiritual ambiance.

Concerts and Cultural Events:

The church is occasionally used as a concert venue, allowing visitors to enjoy classical music performances within its historic walls.

Astronomical Clock:

The southern tower of the church is home to a historical astronomical clock, similar to the one on Prague's Old Town Hall. The clock has a fascinating mechanism and an astronomical dial depicting the positions of celestial bodies.

Historical Context:

The church's history dates back to the 14th century, and it has witnessed significant events in Prague's past, making it a repository of Czech history.

Photography and Views:

The exterior of the church provides a fantastic subject for photography, and its towers offer panoramic views of the Old Town Square and the surrounding area.

Old Town Square Setting:

The Church of Our Lady before Týn is centrally located within the bustling Old Town Square, surrounded by other historic landmarks, shops, cafes, and the vibrant atmosphere of Prague's heart.

Prague Cathedral of Saints Cyril and Methodius

The Prague Cathedral of Saints Cyril and Methodius (Katedrála svatého Cyrila a Metoděje) is a remarkable church with historical significance, located in the New Town (Nové Město) area of Prague. While it may not be as well-known as some of the city's other cathedrals, it holds a unique place in Czech history and is associated with a heroic and poignant event. Here's what you can learn about and experience at the Prague Cathedral of Saints Cyril and Methodius:

Historical Importance:

The cathedral gained international attention during World War II for its role in the assassination of Reinhard Heydrich, a high-ranking Nazi official. Czech resistance fighters carried out the mission, which ultimately led to the church being targeted by the Nazi regime.

Memorial to Czech Heroes:

The church now serves as a memorial to the Czech resistance fighters who were involved in the assassination. The crypt houses a memorial dedicated to the paratroopers who sacrificed their lives for the cause of freedom.

The Operation Anthropoid Story:

The story of Operation Anthropoid, the code name for the assassination mission, is presented through exhibits and displays within the cathedral, offering insight into the bravery and sacrifice of those involved.

Frescoes and Decorations:

The interior of the cathedral features impressive frescoes and decorative elements, creating a solemn and reflective atmosphere.

Jan Palach Memorial:

The cathedral also contains a memorial to Jan Palach, a student who set himself on fire in protest against the Soviet occupation of Czechoslovakia in 1969. His sacrifice is remembered as a symbol of resistance.

Architectural Style:

The cathedral's architecture is influenced by the Neo-Gothic and Art Nouveau styles, adding to its visual appeal and historical context.

Reflection and Contemplation:

Visiting the cathedral offers an opportunity for reflection and contemplation on the sacrifices made by individuals who fought for freedom and against oppression.

Connection to Czech Identity:

The events associated with the Prague Cathedral of Saints Cyril and Methodius are deeply intertwined with Czech national identity and the struggle for independence.

Guided Tours:

Guided tours are often available, providing in-depth information about the cathedral's history, the events of World War II, and the Czech resistance.

Symbol of Resistance:

The cathedral stands as a testament to the resilience and courage of the Czech people in the face of adversity, making it an important historical and cultural landmark.

Church of St. James

The Church of St. James (Kostel svatého Jakuba) is a significant Gothic church located in the heart of Prague's Old Town. With its intriguing history, impressive interior, and unique features, the church holds a special place in the city's architectural and cultural heritage. Here's what you can learn about and experience at the Church of St. James:

Mummified Arm of a Thief:

One of the most curious and well-known aspects of the church is the mummified arm hanging from the ceiling. Legend has it that the thief attempted to steal the jewels from the statue of the Virgin Mary, but the statue miraculously grabbed his arm, preventing the theft.

Gothic Architecture:

The church's Gothic architectural style is characterized by pointed arches, ribbed vaults, and slender columns. Its exterior and interior reflect the grandeur of medieval Gothic design.

Interior Decorations:

The interior of the church features intricate altars, sculptures, and beautiful stained glass windows. The side chapels contain unique and artistic displays.

The Main Altarpiece:

The main altarpiece of the Church of St. James depicts the Assumption of the Virgin Mary and is a masterpiece by renowned Czech artist Karel Škréta.

Historical Significance:

The church has a rich history dating back to the 13th century and has witnessed numerous historical events and cultural changes throughout the centuries.

Holy Stairs:

The church's entrance is graced by a Holy Stairs (Scala Sancta) replica, believed to be a copy of the stairs in Rome that Jesus climbed during his Passion.

Peaceful Atmosphere:

Despite its central location, the Church of St. James provides a peaceful sanctuary away from the bustling city, offering a place for contemplation and prayer.

Cultural Events:

The church occasionally hosts cultural events, including concerts and exhibitions, allowing visitors to experience its unique ambiance in different ways.

Jan Zelivský Memorial:

The church is also associated with the Hussite movement and Jan Zelivský, a prominent Hussite preacher and reformer.

Art and History:

The church's interior is adorned with beautiful artworks and sculptures that provide insights into Prague's artistic and religious heritage.

Basilica of St. Peter and St. Paul

The Basilica of St. Peter and St. Paul (Bazilika svatého Petra a Pavla) is a stunning Neo-Gothic church located atop the

Vyšehrad hill in Prague. This impressive basilica is known for its commanding presence, intricate architectural details, and panoramic views of the city. Here's what you can learn about and experience at the Basilica of St. Peter and St. Paul:

Neo-Gothic Architecture:

The basilica's architecture is characterized by its Neo-Gothic style, with pointed arches, tall spires, and intricate stone carvings. It was built in the late 19th and early 20th centuries, contributing to Prague's rich architectural tapestry.

Iconic Landmark:

The Basilica of St. Peter and St. Paul is one of the most prominent landmarks in Prague, visible from various parts of the city and serving as a symbol of spiritual significance.

Interior Grandeur:

The interior of the basilica is equally impressive, featuring a spacious nave, ornate altars, stained glass windows, and decorative elements that reflect the Neo-Gothic style.

Historical Significance:

The basilica is located within the Vyšehrad fortress complex, an area with historical and cultural significance. It is also the final resting place of several notable Czech artists, musicians, and public figures.

Views from the Tower:

Visitors have the opportunity to climb the basilica's tower for panoramic views of Prague. The ascent provides a breathtaking vantage point to admire the city's skyline and the Vltava River.

Vyšehrad Cemetery:

The basilica is surrounded by the Vyšehrad Cemetery, where many prominent Czech personalities are buried. Notable figures include composers Antonín Dvořák and Bedřich Smetana, as well as writer Karel Čapek.

Cultural Events:

The basilica occasionally hosts cultural events, including classical music concerts and performances, creating a unique setting to enjoy artistic expressions.

Peaceful Setting:

The basilica's hilltop location offers a serene and peaceful environment away from the city's hustle and bustle, making it an ideal place for quiet contemplation.

Spiritual Experience:

The basilica is a place of worship, offering regular religious services and providing visitors with an opportunity for reflection and connection with their spirituality.

Architectural Details:

Take time to admire the intricate details of the basilica's architecture, from the fine stonework on the exterior to the delicate ornamentation within the interior.

Church of Our Lady Victorious

The Church of Our Lady Victorious (Kostel Panny Marie Vítězné) is a charming Baroque church located in Prague's Lesser Quarter (Malá Strana). While relatively small in size, it holds great significance as the home of the famous Infant Jesus of Prague statue, a beloved religious icon that attracts pilgrims and visitors from around the world. Here's what you can learn about and experience at the Church of Our Lady Victorious:

Infant Jesus of Prague:

The church is most famous for housing the Infant Jesus of Prague statue, a wooden sculpture of the child Jesus that holds deep spiritual and devotional meaning for many people. The statue is known for its ornate and varied vestments, which are changed regularly throughout the year.

Baroque Architecture:

The church's Baroque architecture is characterized by its ornate facade, decorative elements, and elaborate interior design. It reflects the opulence and artistic style of the Baroque period.

Relics and Altars:

In addition to the Infant Jesus of Prague statue, the church contains other altars and religious artifacts that are intricately adorned and offer spaces for prayer and contemplation.

Peaceful Ambiance:

The Church of Our Lady Victorious provides a serene and tranquil atmosphere, allowing visitors to escape the bustling streets of Prague and find a moment of quiet reflection.

Pilgrimage Site:

The church attracts pilgrims from various parts of the world who come to venerate the Infant Jesus of Prague statue and seek spiritual blessings.

Spiritual Retreat:

Visitors are welcome to attend religious services, including Mass, within the church, providing an opportunity to participate in worship and connect with the local faith community.

Gift Shop:

The church often has a gift shop where you can purchase devotional items, souvenirs, and replicas of the Infant Jesus statue.

Historical Context:

The church's history dates back to the 17th century, and it has witnessed centuries of religious and cultural developments in Prague.

Artistic Details:

Take time to appreciate the intricate details of the church's interior, including the altars, sculptures, and decorative elements that contribute to its beauty.

Devotion and Faith:

Whether you are a religious pilgrim or a curious traveler, the Church of Our Lady Victorious offers an opportunity to witness the devotion and faith of individuals who come to honor the Infant Jesus of Prague.

St. Giles' Church (Kostel svatého Jiljí)

St. Giles' Church (Kostel svatého Jiljí) is a historic religious building located in the heart of Prague's Old Town. This Romanesque church, known for its architectural significance and artistic treasures, offers visitors a glimpse into Prague's rich history and cultural heritage. Here's what you can learn about and experience at St. Giles' Church:

Romanesque Architecture:

St. Giles' Church is a notable example of Romanesque architecture in Prague. The church's design features rounded arches, thick walls, and simple yet elegant geometric patterns.

Tranquil Atmosphere:

Despite its central location, the church offers a peaceful and quiet environment, making it a welcoming place for contemplation and prayer.

Interior Frescoes:

The interior of the church is adorned with well-preserved frescoes that depict scenes from the life of St. Giles, as well as other religious and biblical subjects.

Baroque Alterations:

Over the centuries, St. Giles' Church underwent Baroque modifications, adding decorative elements, altars, and statues that reflect the ornate style of that period.

Jan Hus Connection:

St. Giles' Church is associated with Jan Hus, an important figure in Czech history and the Protestant Reformation. The church's pulpit is believed to have been used by Hus for his sermons.

Wooden Statues:

The church houses a collection of wooden statues and sculptures, including figures of saints and angels, contributing to the overall artistic atmosphere.

Historical Landmark:

The church's origins date back to the 13th century, and it has witnessed various historical events, making it a living testament to Prague's past.

Spiritual Significance:

St. Giles' Church continues to hold regular religious services, providing visitors with an opportunity to attend Mass and connect with the local faith community.

Architectural Details:

Take time to admire the architectural details of the church, including its arched doorways, stone carvings, and the simple yet elegant layout that defines the Romanesque style.

Peaceful Retreat:

Visiting St. Giles' Church offers a chance to escape the urban hustle and bustle and immerse yourself in the tranquil ambiance of this historic sanctuary.

GALLERIES AND MUSEUMS

Prague, the capital of the Czech Republic, is a city rich in history, culture, and art. It boasts numerous galleries and museums that offer a glimpse into the country's past, as well as contemporary art scenes. Here's a guide to some of the top galleries and museums to explore during your visit to Prague:

National Gallery in Prague (Národní galerie v Praze)

The National Gallery in Prague (Národní galerie v Praze) is the most prominent and comprehensive art institution in the Czech Republic. It houses an extensive collection of artworks spanning from the Middle Ages to the present day. The gallery is spread across various locations in Prague, each offering a unique perspective on the country's artistic heritage. Here are some key locations and highlights within the National Gallery:

Veletržní Palace:

This modernist building is home to the National Gallery's collection of 19th, 20th, and 21st-century art. The collection features works by Czech and international artists, including pieces by Pablo Picasso, Vincent van Gogh, František Kupka, and Alfons Mucha. The impressive collection of modern and contemporary art spans various movements, from Cubism to Surrealism and beyond.

Old Royal Palace (Starý královský palác):

Located within Prague Castle, the Old Royal Palace features historical art and artifacts. The Vladislav Hall within the palace showcases the monumental 16th-century painting "The Battle of White Mountain" by Pieter Schoubroeck.

Schwarzenberg Palace (Švihovský palác):

Situated in the heart of Prague, this palace is known for its Baroque architecture and houses an impressive collection of European art from the Baroque era. The collection includes works by famous artists such as Peter Paul Rubens and Anthony van Dyck.

Convent of St. Agnes of Bohemia (Klášter sv. Anežky České):

This medieval building serves as a home for the National Gallery's collection of medieval and early Renaissance art. The collection includes Gothic and Romanesque artworks, altarpieces, sculptures, and illuminated manuscripts.

Trade Fair Palace (Palác Kinských):

This functionalist building houses a diverse range of temporary exhibitions, often featuring international contemporary art. It offers a dynamic space for modern and experimental art installations.

Salm Palace (Šternberský palác):

Part of the National Gallery, this palace focuses on European art from the Renaissance to the Baroque period. The collection includes works by Titian, El Greco, and Lucas Cranach the Elder.

National Museum (Národní muzeum)

The National Museum (Národní muzeum) in Prague is a major cultural institution in the Czech Republic dedicated to preserving and showcasing the country's natural and cultural heritage. It is housed in a magnificent neo-Renaissance building located at the top of Wenceslas Square, one of Prague's main thoroughfares. The museum's diverse collections cover a wide range of topics, from natural history and anthropology to art and history. Here's what you can expect to find at the National Museum:

Exhibitions:

The museum's permanent exhibitions are spread across several buildings and cover various themes, including paleontology, mineralogy, zoology, anthropology, history, and art. The Historical Building focuses on Czech history and features artifacts from ancient times to the 20th century. The New Building hosts exhibitions related to natural history and science.

Paleontological and Geological Collections:

The National Museum is renowned for its extensive collection of fossils, minerals, and geological specimens, providing insights into the Earth's history and evolution.

Anthropological Exhibits:

The museum's anthropological collections include artifacts from cultures around the world, offering insights into human history, societies, and traditions.

Historical Artifacts:

The Historical Building features exhibits that showcase the history of the Czech lands, including medieval artifacts, historical documents, and items from significant events.

Czech Cubism Collection:

The National Museum also boasts a notable collection of Czech Cubist art, which is a unique local artistic movement from the early 20th century.

Educational Programs and Events:

The National Museum offers a variety of educational programs, workshops, lectures, and special events for visitors of all ages, making it an engaging destination for families and students.

Panoramic Views:

Visitors can enjoy panoramic views of Wenceslas Square and the surrounding area from the top of the museum's dome.

DOX Centre for Contemporary Art

The DOX Centre for Contemporary Art is a prominent contemporary art institution located in Prague, Czech Republic. It is known for its dedication to presenting cutting-edge contemporary art exhibitions, installations, and interdisciplinary projects. Founded in 2008, DOX has become a hub for both Czech and international contemporary artists to showcase their work. Here's what you can expect to find at the DOX Centre:

Exhibitions and Installations:

DOX features a dynamic program of temporary exhibitions that cover a wide range of contemporary art forms, including visual arts, multimedia, photography, sculpture, video art, and more. The exhibitions often explore social, cultural, political, and environmental themes, fostering dialogue and reflection.

Multimedia and Interdisciplinary Projects:

DOX is known for its innovative approach, often hosting multimedia and interdisciplinary projects that blend art, technology, and other fields. These projects can include performances, workshops, and interactive installations.

Czech and International Artists:

The center supports both emerging and established artists, providing them with a platform to experiment and showcase their work to a diverse audience.

Café and Bookstore:

DOX offers a café where visitors can relax and discuss the exhibitions they've seen. The museum also has a bookstore that features a curated selection of art books, catalogs, and publications.

Educational Programs and Events:

DOX regularly organizes educational programs, workshops, lectures, discussions, and screenings, creating opportunities for visitors to engage with the art and artists on a deeper level.

Architecture and Design:

The DOX building itself is a work of art, featuring innovative architecture and design. The spacious galleries, open spaces, and industrial aesthetic contribute to the center's unique atmosphere.

Cultural Events and Festivals:

Throughout the year, DOX hosts cultural events, film screenings, music performances, and festivals that complement the contemporary art experience.

Museum of Communism

The Museum of Communism is a unique historical museum located in Prague, Czech Republic. It offers visitors a comprehensive and engaging insight into the era of communist rule in Czechoslovakia, particularly during the 20th century. The museum's exhibits and displays provide a glimpse into the political, social, and cultural aspects of life under communist rule. Here's what you can expect to find at the Museum of Communism:

Exhibitions and Artifacts:

The museum features a diverse collection of artifacts, photographs, documents, and multimedia displays that chronicle the history of communism in Czechoslovakia. Exhibitions cover key moments, figures, and events from the communist era, including the rise of the Communist Party, daily life, propaganda, secret police activities, and the Velvet Revolution.

Propaganda and Ideology:

The museum explores the role of propaganda in shaping public perception and the dissemination of communist ideology. Visitors can see various propaganda materials, posters, and objects that were used to promote the regime's messages.

Interactivity and Multimedia:

The exhibits often use multimedia elements, including videos, interactive displays, and audio recordings, to enhance the learning experience and provide a more immersive understanding of the historical context.

Reconstructed Environments:

Some parts of the museum recreate typical settings from the communist period, such as a classroom, an interrogation room, and a grocery store, giving visitors a sense of the everyday life during that time.

Historical Context and Analysis:

The museum provides historical context and analysis through informative panels and displays, helping visitors understand the broader socio-political background of the era.

Velvet Revolution and Post-Communist Era:

The museum also covers the events of the Velvet Revolution in 1989, which marked the peaceful transition from communism to democracy in Czechoslovakia.

Gift Shop and Café:

The Museum of Communism includes a gift shop where visitors can purchase books, souvenirs, and items related to Czech history and culture. There is also a café where visitors can relax after exploring the exhibits.

Kampa Museum

The Kampa Museum (Muzeum Kampa) is a contemporary art museum located on Kampa Island in Prague, Czech Republic. Situated in a charming location near the Vltava River, the museum focuses on modern European and Czech art from the 20th and 21st centuries. It's known for its diverse collection and exhibitions, as well as its dedication to showcasing the work of both established and emerging artists. Here's what you can expect to find at the Kampa Museum:

Collections and Exhibitions:

The museum's permanent collection features a wide range of artworks, including paintings, sculptures, photography, and other visual arts forms.

The collection includes works by prominent Czech artists, as well as international figures, offering visitors a comprehensive look at modern and contemporary art.

Czech Modern Art:

The museum places a strong emphasis on Czech modern art and showcases works by renowned artists like František Kupka, Emil Filla, and Otto Gutfreund.

International Contemporary Art:

In addition to Czech artists, the museum often hosts exhibitions of contemporary art by international artists, contributing to a global perspective on artistic trends.

Temporary Exhibitions:

The Kampa Museum regularly hosts temporary exhibitions that cover a diverse range of artistic styles, movements, and themes.

Café and Garden:

The museum features a café and outdoor garden area, providing visitors with a relaxing space to enjoy refreshments and scenic views of the Vltava River and surrounding area.

Cultural Events and Programs:

Kampa Museum often organizes cultural events, lectures, workshops, and film screenings to engage visitors and promote dialogue about contemporary art and culture.

Kampa Park Sculptures:

Outside the museum, you'll find a park area with various sculptures, creating a unique blend of art and nature.

Architecture and Location:

The museum itself is housed in a historic mill building, adding to its unique character. Its location on Kampa Island provides a tranquil escape from the bustling city.

Franz Kafka Museum

The Franz Kafka Museum is a museum dedicated to the life and work of the renowned Czech writer Franz Kafka. Located in Prague, Czech Republic, the museum provides an immersive and insightful experience into Kafka's literary contributions, personal life, and the historical and cultural context in which he lived. Here's what you can expect to find at the Franz Kafka Museum:

Exhibitions and Displays:

The museum features a wide range of exhibits, documents, manuscripts, letters, and personal belongings related to Franz Kafka.

Visitors can explore Kafka's literary creations, including some of his most famous works like "The Metamorphosis," "The Trial," and "The Castle."

Biographical Insights:

The museum delves into Kafka's life, family background, relationships, and struggles, providing a deeper understanding of the man behind the iconic literature.

Interactive and Multimedia Elements:

The museum employs interactive and multimedia installations to engage visitors and create a more immersive experience. These elements help convey Kafka's themes and ideas in a dynamic way.

Quotes and Philosophy:

The museum prominently features Kafka's quotes and philosophical thoughts, allowing visitors to explore his complex and introspective mind.

Contextualizing Kafka's Work:

The exhibits aim to contextualize Kafka's work within the social, political, and cultural environment of his time, highlighting how his writings resonate with broader themes and historical events.

Temporary Exhibitions and Events:

The museum often hosts temporary exhibitions, lectures, readings, and other events related to literature, Kafka, and his legacy.

Gift Shop and Café:

The museum offers a gift shop where visitors can find Kafka-related books, souvenirs, and memorabilia. There's also a café where you can relax and reflect on your visit.

Memorial Sculpture:

Outside the museum, you'll find the famous kinetic sculpture "Piss" by artist David Černý, which is a playful homage to Kafka.

Lobkowicz Palace

Lobkowicz Palace (Lobkowický palác) is a historic palace located within the Prague Castle complex in Prague, Czech Republic. It is a significant cultural and historical site that houses the Lobkowicz Collections, one of the oldest, largest, and most important private art collections in Central Europe. The palace offers visitors a unique opportunity to explore centuries of European history, art, and culture. Here's what you can expect to find at Lobkowicz Palace:

Lobkowicz Collections:

The palace is renowned for its extensive art collections, which include paintings, decorative arts, historical artifacts, musical instruments, manuscripts, and rare books. The collections encompass a wide range of periods and styles, from Renaissance and Baroque to Classical and Romantic.

Art and Decorative Arts:

Visitors can admire works by renowned artists such as Canaletto, Bruegel the Elder, Velázquez, and Cranach the Elder, among others. The palace's exquisite interior is adorned with intricate decorative arts, including ceramics, porcelain, furniture, and textiles.

Musical Instruments and Manuscripts:

The palace houses an exceptional collection of musical instruments, including pieces by famous composers such as Beethoven and Mozart.

The manuscript collection includes original scores by Beethoven, Mozart, and other composers, providing insight into their creative processes.

Self-Guided Tours:

Visitors can explore the palace at their own pace with self-guided audio tours that provide in-depth information about the artworks, historical significance, and the Lobkowicz family.

Concerts and Events:

Lobkowicz Palace hosts classical music concerts in its stunning concert halls, offering a unique opportunity to experience live music within a historical setting.

Views and Atmosphere:

The palace's location within the Prague Castle complex provides panoramic views of the city and the Vltava River, creating a picturesque backdrop for your visit.

Café and Gift Shop:

The palace features a café where you can enjoy refreshments and a gift shop offering souvenirs, books, and other items related to the palace and its collections.

Museum of Decorative Arts

The Museum of Decorative Arts (Uměleckoprůmyslové museum) in Prague, Czech Republic, is a prominent cultural institution dedicated to the preservation and exhibition of decorative arts, design, and craftsmanship. Established in the late 19th century, the museum showcases a diverse collection of objects that highlight the artistic and functional aspects of various historical periods and cultural contexts. Here's what you can expect to find at the Museum of Decorative Arts:

Collections and Exhibitions:

The museum's collections encompass a wide range of decorative arts, including furniture, ceramics, glassware, textiles, jewelry, metalwork, and more. Exhibitions feature both historical and contemporary pieces, providing insights into different styles, techniques, and cultural influences.

Czech and International Artistry:

The museum emphasizes Czech decorative arts and craftsmanship, showcasing works by local artists and designers. Visitors can also explore international pieces, allowing them to compare and contrast different artistic traditions and trends.

Historical Periods and Styles:

The museum's collections span various historical periods, from Gothic and Renaissance to Art Nouveau and Art Deco. The exhibits provide a visual timeline of artistic evolution and reflect the changing tastes and aesthetics of different eras.

Design and Innovation:

The museum highlights the role of design and innovation in decorative arts, exploring how artists and artisans have pushed the boundaries of materials and techniques.

Educational Programs and Workshops:

The museum offers educational programs, workshops, and lectures that provide deeper insights into the decorative arts, design principles, and historical contexts.

Temporary Exhibitions:

In addition to its permanent collections, the museum hosts temporary exhibitions that focus on specific themes, artists, or design movements.

Café and Gift Shop:

The Museum of Decorative Arts typically includes a café where visitors can enjoy refreshments, and a gift shop offering a variety of design-related items and souvenirs.

Chicagoland Czech American Community Center

The Chicagoland Czech American Community Center (CCACC) is a cultural and social institution located in the Chicago metropolitan area, specifically in the United States. The center serves as a hub for individuals of Czech and Slovak heritage, providing a space for community events, cultural activities, and the preservation of Czech and Slovak traditions. Here's an overview of the Chicagoland Czech American Community Center:

Purpose and Mission:

The CCACC aims to connect and celebrate the Czech and Slovak American communities in the Chicagoland area. It serves as a place where individuals with Czech and Slovak heritage can come together, learn about their cultural roots, and engage in various cultural and social activities.

Cultural Events and Activities:

The center organizes and hosts a variety of cultural events and activities, such as traditional dances, music performances, festivals, lectures, workshops, and art exhibitions. These events help promote and preserve Czech and Slovak heritage while also sharing it with the broader community.

Community Involvement:

The CCACC fosters a sense of community among Czech and Slovak Americans by providing opportunities for people to connect, share stories, and celebrate their shared heritage. It's a space where individuals can find like-minded people and participate in events that honor their cultural background.

Language and Education:

The center may offer language classes and educational programs related to Czech and Slovak languages, history, and traditions. This can be especially valuable for younger generations who want to learn more about their heritage.

Heritage Preservation:

One of the main goals of the CCACC is to preserve and promote Czech and Slovak heritage for future generations. By hosting cultural events, workshops, and exhibitions, the center contributes to the ongoing vitality of these traditions.

Culinary Offerings:

Czech and Slovak cuisine often play a central role in cultural events and gatherings organized by the CCACC. Traditional dishes and recipes may be showcased during festivals and special occasions.

Networking and Socializing:

The center provides an environment where people can socialize, network, and make meaningful connections with others who share similar cultural backgrounds.

Location and Accessibility:

The specific location of the Chicagoland Czech American Community Center may vary, so it's recommended to check their official website or contact them directly for the most up-to-date information.

Membership and Support:

The CCACC might offer membership opportunities for individuals interested in supporting and actively participating in their activities. Membership can include benefits such as access to events, newsletters, and special discounts.

Cultural Exchange:

The center may also facilitate cultural exchange programs, welcoming visitors from the Czech and Slovak Republics and promoting a sense of global connection within the Czech and Slovak diaspora.

CUISINES

Prague's cuisine is a delightful blend of traditional Czech dishes and international influences, reflecting the city's rich history and diverse cultural connections. From hearty comfort food to modern gastronomic creations, Prague offers a range of culinary experiences that cater to various tastes. Here are some highlights of Prague's cuisine:

Czech Specialities

Czech cuisine is known for its hearty and flavorful dishes that reflect the country's history, culture, and agricultural heritage. Here are some classic Czech specialties that you must try when visiting Prague and other parts of the Czech Republic:

Svíčková na smetaně:

A signature Czech dish made from marinated beef sirloin served with a creamy sauce made from vegetables, cream, and spices. It's often accompanied by cranberry sauce and topped with whipped cream.

Vepřo-knedlo-zelo:

Roast pork (vepřová pečeně) served with knedlíky (dumplings) and sauerkraut (zelí). This dish is a quintessential Czech comfort food.

Bramboráky:

Potato pancakes made from grated potatoes, flour, and seasonings. They are often served as a side dish or appetizer and are especially popular during outdoor events and festivals.

Guláš:

A rich and hearty beef or pork stew made with onions, paprika, and spices. It's typically served with knedlíky (dumplings) or bread.

Trdelník:

A sweet pastry made from rolled dough that is wrapped around a stick, grilled, and coated with sugar and cinnamon. It's a popular street food and dessert.

Uzené:

Smoked meats, particularly sausages and ham, are commonly enjoyed as part of Czech cuisine. They are often served with bread and mustard.

Smažený sýr:

Fried cheese, typically Edam or Hermelín cheese, coated in breadcrumbs and deep-fried until golden and crispy. It's often served with tartar sauce and a side salad.

Nakládaný hermelín:

Pickled Hermelín cheese, marinated with garlic, peppers, and spices, and served as an appetizer or snack.

Kuba:

A traditional dish made from cooked barley mixed with mushrooms, onions, and often smoked meat. It's a comforting and filling option.

Koláče:

Sweet pastries filled with various fillings, such as fruit, poppy seeds, or sweetened cheese. They are popular as breakfast treats or desserts.

Palačinky:

Czech-style crepes that can be filled with sweet fillings like jam, fruit, or chocolate, or savory fillings like ham and cheese.

Česnečka:

A garlic soup made with garlic, potatoes, and often topped with croutons and grated cheese. It's a popular choice for curing hangovers.

Chlebíčky:

Open-faced sandwiches with various toppings, often served as appetizers during social gatherings.

Tvarohovník:

A cottage cheese-based dessert or snack, sometimes baked in a pastry shell and flavored with vanilla or fruit.

Street Food

Prague's street food scene has grown in popularity in recent years, offering a diverse range of delicious and convenient options for both locals and visitors. From traditional Czech bites to international flavors, here are some popular street food items you can enjoy while exploring the city:

Trdelník:

A beloved Czech sweet treat, trdelník is a rolled dough pastry that's wrapped around a stick, grilled, and coated with sugar, cinnamon, and nuts. It's a popular choice for a quick and satisfying dessert.

Sausages (klobása):

Grilled sausages, often served in a bun or with a side of mustard, are a classic street food option that you'll find at food stalls and markets throughout the city.

Langos:

A Hungarian-inspired delight, langos is deep-fried dough topped with various toppings like garlic, cheese, and ketchup. It's a savory and indulgent snack.

Chlebíčky:

These open-faced sandwiches are a staple of Czech cuisine and come in various combinations, featuring toppings like ham, egg, cheese, vegetables, and spreads.

Bramboráky:

Potato pancakes are a comforting and flavorful choice, often served with garlic sauce or ketchup. They make for a delicious snack or light meal.

Fried Cheese (smažený sýr):

Indulge in a deep-fried cheese sandwich, typically served with a side salad and tartar sauce. It's a popular option for both locals and tourists.

Klobásky:

Another type of Czech sausage, klobásky are often enjoyed at outdoor events and festivals. They can be served in a bun or on their own.

Palačinky:

These thin Czech-style crepes are filled with sweet fillings like Nutella, fruit, or whipped cream. They're perfect for satisfying your sweet tooth.

Goulash:

Experience the Czech version of this hearty stew, served in a bread bowl for a warm and satisfying meal on the go.

Falafel:

Prague's diverse food scene includes international options like falafel wraps, which are a favorite among those looking for a vegetarian or vegan street food choice.

Pizza Slices:

You'll find food stalls offering generous slices of pizza, with various toppings to choose from.

Kebabs:

Enjoy a classic kebab wrap, filled with grilled meat, vegetables, and your choice of sauces.

Asian Street Food:

Some areas of Prague offer a variety of Asian street food options, including dumplings, bao buns, and noodle dishes.

Ice Cream and Gelato:

On a hot day, indulge in a scoop of creamy gelato or Czech-style ice cream from a local ice cream shop.

Food Markets

Prague is home to several vibrant food markets where you can immerse yourself in the local food scene, sample traditional Czech delicacies, and explore a variety of fresh produce, artisanal products, and street food. Here are some of the popular food markets in Prague:

Havelské Tržiště (Havelska Market):

Located in the heart of Old Town, Havelské Tržiště is one of the oldest markets in Prague. You'll find stalls selling fruits, vegetables, flowers, crafts, and souvenirs. It's a great place to experience the atmosphere of a traditional market.

Náplavka Farmers' Market:

Náplavka is a lively farmers' market held along the Vltava River. It offers a wide range of local products, including fresh produce, bread, pastries, meats, cheeses, and beverages. The market also hosts food stalls and a relaxed, riverside setting.

Jiřák Farmers' Market:

Located in the Vinohrady district, Jiřák Farmers' Market is known for its high-quality local and organic products. You can find fresh fruits, vegetables, meats, dairy products, baked goods, and more. The market's atmosphere is bustling and friendly.

Prague Market Hall (Pražská tržnice):

The Prague Market Hall is a modern food market with a diverse range of stalls, including fresh produce, meats, fish, cheese, spices, and international ingredients. It's a great place to explore various culinary offerings.

Kulaťák Farmers' Market:

This market is situated in the Dejvice district and offers a selection of fresh produce, artisanal products, and street food. It's a popular spot for both locals and visitors looking for high-quality ingredients.

Florenc Market:

Florenc Market is located near the main bus station and offers a variety of food stalls and vendors. You'll find fresh produce, meats, cheeses, and other grocery items, as well as a few eateries.

Holešovice Market:

Holešovice Market is a modern food hall with a mix of traditional Czech and international cuisine. It's a great place to try different flavors and enjoy a meal in a lively environment.

Anděl Farmers' Market:

This market is located near the Anděl metro station and features stalls selling fresh produce, baked goods, meats, cheeses, and other artisanal products.

Kulaťák Food Bazaar:

A food market in Prague 6, Kulaťák Food Bazaar offers a variety of street food options and fresh ingredients for cooking at home.

Best Restaurants to Try

Prague boasts a diverse culinary scene, offering a wide range of dining options from traditional Czech cuisine to international flavors and innovative gastronomy. Here are some of the best restaurants in Prague where you can savor delicious dishes and enjoy memorable dining experiences:

La Degustation Bohême Bourgeoise:

This Michelin-starred restaurant focuses on modern interpretations of traditional Czech dishes. It offers tasting menus that showcase the flavors and ingredients of Czech cuisine in an elegant setting.

Field:

Another Michelin-starred gem, Field offers creative and seasonal cuisine with a focus on locally sourced ingredients. The menu changes frequently, providing a fresh dining experience each visit.

Lokál Dlouhááá:

Lokál is a popular chain of Czech pubs with a focus on traditional Czech cuisine and beer. Lokál Dlouhááá is known for its hearty and authentic dishes served in a casual and lively atmosphere.

CottoCrudo:

Located in the Four Seasons Hotel, CottoCrudo offers a mix of Italian and Mediterranean cuisine with a modern twist. The restaurant emphasizes high-quality ingredients and offers an extensive wine list.

Sansho:

Sansho is a trendy and dynamic restaurant known for its fusion of Asian and European flavors. The ever-changing menu features creative dishes with a focus on fresh ingredients and bold flavors.

La Finestra:

La Finestra is a steakhouse and bistro that specializes in top-quality meat and seasonal ingredients. The restaurant offers a wide range of cuts and cooking styles, along with a selection of Italian wines.

Kuchyň:

Kuchyň is a cozy and welcoming eatery that offers a daily changing menu of Czech comfort food and international dishes. It's a great place to experience homemade cooking in a relaxed environment.

Eska:

Eska is a modern bistro and bakery known for its emphasis on locally sourced ingredients and house-made products. The menu offers a mix of traditional Czech dishes and innovative creations.

Bellevue Restaurant:

Set in a beautiful historic building with views of Prague Castle and Charles Bridge, Bellevue Restaurant offers a fine dining experience with a menu that combines Czech and international flavors.

T-Anker Rooftop Restaurant:

For panoramic views of Prague's Old Town, head to T-Anker Rooftop Restaurant. The menu features a variety of dishes, and the rooftop terrace is a popular spot for both dining and drinks.

PRAGUE'S UNDERGROUND

Prague's underground is a fascinating and often lesser-explored aspect of the city's history and culture. Beneath the bustling streets and historic buildings, there lies a network of hidden passages, cellars, tunnels, and crypts that offer insights into the city's past. Here are some intriguing aspects of Prague's underground that you might find intriguing:

Underground Passages and Cellars

Many of Prague's historical buildings have hidden cellars and underground passages that were once used for storage, trade, and even secret meetings. Some of these passages have been preserved and can be explored on guided tours, offering a unique perspective on the city's architecture and development.

Prague Castle Subterranean Spaces

Prague Castle, the city's iconic landmark, has its own network of underground spaces, including tunnels, cellars, and chambers. These spaces were historically used for various purposes, such as storing supplies and conducting rituals. Some parts of the castle's underground can be visited on guided tours.

Vyšehrad Casemates

Vyšehrad, another historic fortress in Prague, has a series of underground casemates that were once used as defense fortifications. Visitors can explore these dark and atmospheric spaces to learn about their historical significance.

Torture and Execution Chambers

Prague's dark history includes tales of medieval dungeons and torture chambers. While some of these stories might be embellished, some underground areas in Prague have been associated with past practices of punishment and execution.

Alchemists' Workshops

Prague has a history of alchemical experimentation, and some underground spaces are said to have been used as alchemists' workshops. These spaces can be explored on themed tours that delve into the mysteries of alchemy.

Crypts and Burial Sites

Beneath several churches in Prague, you can find crypts and burial sites that house the remains of historical figures, nobility, and religious figures. These crypts provide a glimpse into the city's religious and social history.

Underground Historical Exhibitions

Some underground spaces have been converted into museums and exhibitions that offer insights into different aspects of Prague's history, from medieval times to the modern era.

Ghost Tours and Paranormal Activities

Prague's underground has also become the setting for ghost tours and paranormal-themed experiences, where you can learn about legends and spooky stories associated with the city's subterranean world.

Art and Cultural Spaces

Some underground areas have been repurposed as art galleries, cultural venues, and performance spaces. These unique locations host exhibitions, concerts, and events that add a creative twist to Prague's underground scene.

SPORT CULTURE

Sports culture in Prague is a vibrant and integral part of the city's social fabric. Prague residents have a strong passion for sports, and the city offers a wide range of sporting activities, events, and venues that cater to both participants and spectators. Here's a glimpse into Prague's sports culture:

Strahov Stadium

Strahov Stadium, officially known as the Strahovský stadion, is a historic sports stadium located on Strahov Hill in Prague, Czech Republic. It is one of the largest stadiums in the world in terms of seating capacity and holds a special place in the city's sports history. Here's an overview of Strahov Stadium:

Historical Significance:

Strahov Stadium was built in the 1920s and 1930s as part of a sports complex that included various sports facilities and training areas. It was designed to showcase the Czech nation's love for sports and physical activities.

Impressive Capacity:

Strahov Stadium has an astonishing seating capacity that can accommodate up to around 220,000 spectators. While this capacity is rarely filled nowadays, the stadium's grandeur and size are still awe-inspiring.

Athletic Events and Performances:

The stadium was originally used for various athletic events, including track and field competitions, as well as gymnastics and other sports. It was also used for mass gymnastic displays and performances, reflecting the importance of physical culture during that era.

Architecture and Design:

The stadium features an Art Deco architectural style and is characterized by its imposing presence, wide stands, and sweeping views of the city. It has a distinct horseshoe shape and includes an iconic tower at its entrance.

Decline and Modern Use:

In the latter half of the 20th century, Strahov Stadium fell into disuse and disrepair. The massive seating capacity became impractical for modern sports events. However, the stadium continues to host occasional events, including concerts and cultural performances.

Tours and Visits:

While the stadium may not be in regular use for sports events, visitors to Prague can still explore the exterior of the stadium and take guided tours that provide insight into its history and significance. The tower offers panoramic views of Prague.

Nearby Attractions:

Strahov Stadium is located near other notable attractions, including the Strahov Monastery and its impressive library, which houses a vast collection of books and manuscripts.

Symbol of Czech Sports Culture:

Strahov Stadium remains a symbol of Czech sports culture and a reminder of the country's historic dedication to physical fitness and athleticism.

Ice Hockey

Ice hockey is a beloved sport in Prague and the Czech Republic as a whole. The city has a rich ice hockey history, with local teams like HC Sparta Prague and HC Slavia Prague competing in the top leagues.

Football (Soccer)

Football is immensely popular in Prague, with several football clubs based in the city. AC Sparta Prague and SK Slavia Prague are two of the most notable football clubs with passionate fan bases.

Running and Marathons

Prague hosts various running events and marathons throughout the year, attracting both local and international participants. The Prague International Marathon is a major highlight on the city's sports calendar.

Cycling

Prague offers scenic routes for cyclists, including paths along the Vltava River and through picturesque neighborhoods. Cycling is a popular recreational activity, and the city also hosts cycling races and events.

Tennis

Tennis is a well-loved sport in Prague, and the city boasts numerous tennis courts and clubs where enthusiasts can play and compete. The Prague Open is a notable tennis tournament held in the city.

Basketball

Basketball has a growing presence in Prague, with several basketball clubs and leagues. The city hosts matches and tournaments, providing opportunities for both players and fans.

Water Sports

The Vltava River provides a backdrop for water sports such as rowing, kayaking, and paddleboarding. Clubs and centers offer lessons and equipment rental for those interested in water-based activities.

DAY TRIPS FROM PRAGUE

Prague is surrounded by beautiful landscapes, charming towns, and historical sites that make for excellent day trips. If you're looking to explore beyond the city, here are some popular day trip destinations you can consider:

Kutná Hora

Known for its stunning Gothic architecture and the famous Sedlec Ossuary (Bone Church), Kutná Hora is a UNESCO World Heritage Site located about an hour's train ride from Prague.

Český Krumlov

This picturesque town is famous for its well-preserved medieval architecture, narrow winding streets, and Český Krumlov Castle. It's located approximately three hours from Prague.

Karlštejn Castle

Just a short train ride from Prague, Karlštejn Castle is a 14th-century fortress nestled in the Czech countryside. It's known for its impressive architecture and beautiful surroundings.

Terezín (Theresienstadt)

A sobering historical site, Terezín was a former Nazi concentration camp and ghetto during World War II. It's about an hour's drive from Prague and offers insight into the city's dark history.

Plzeň (Pilsen)

Known as the birthplace of Pilsner beer, Plzeň is home to the Pilsner Urquell Brewery. You can tour the brewery and learn about the beer-making process. It's about an hour and a half from Prague.

Konopiště Castle

This historic castle is famous for being the former residence of Archduke Franz Ferdinand of Austria. It's surrounded by beautiful gardens and is located about an hour from Prague.

Karlovy Vary (Carlsbad)

A renowned spa town, Karlovy Vary is known for its hot springs and beautiful architecture. It's about two hours from Prague and offers a relaxing day getaway.

Bohemian Switzerland National Park

If you're a nature enthusiast, consider a trip to this stunning national park known for its dramatic sandstone formations and breathtaking landscapes. It's about two and a half hours from Prague.

Dresden, Germany

Cross the border to visit Dresden, a German city known for its impressive architecture, including the Frauenkirche and Zwinger Palace. It's about two hours from Prague.

Brno

The second-largest city in the Czech Republic, Brno offers a mix of historical sites, modern culture, and vibrant nightlife. It's about two and a half hours from Prague.

DAY ITINERARIES

Here are 10 suggested itineraries for day trips from Prague, each focusing on a different aspect of the region's history, culture, and natural beauty:

Kutná Hora Historical Tour

- Visit the UNESCO-listed town of Kutná Hora.
- Explore the Gothic St. Barbara's Church and the Italian Court.
- Tour the unique Sedlec Ossuary (Bone Church).
- **Duration:** Full day.

Český Krumlov and Castle Adventure

- Explore the charming town of Český Krumlov with its medieval architecture.
- Visit Český Krumlov Castle and enjoy panoramic views.
- Stroll along the Vltava River and explore the town's galleries and shops.

- **Duration:** Full day.

Karlštejn Castle and Nature Escape

- Discover Karlštejn Castle's impressive architecture and history.
- Enjoy a scenic hike in the surrounding countryside.
- Visit local cafes and shops in the nearby village.
- **Duration:** Full day.

Terezín Holocaust Memorial Tour

- Visit the Terezín Ghetto and Concentration Camp Memorial.
- Learn about the history of the site during World War II.
- Reflect on the tragic events that occurred here.
- **Duration:** Half to full day.

Pilsen Beer and Culture Experience

- Take a brewery tour at Pilsner Urquell Brewery.
- Explore the historic center of Pilsen.
- Visit the Great Synagogue and Pilsen's museums.
- **Duration:** Full day.

Karlovy Vary Spa Retreat

- Relax in the famous hot springs and spas of Karlovy Vary.
- Stroll along the elegant colonnades and taste the local spa wafers.
- Visit the Moser Glassworks and enjoy the picturesque surroundings.
- **Duration:** Full day.

Bohemian Switzerland Hiking Adventure

- Hike through the stunning landscapes of Bohemian Switzerland National Park.
- Explore Pravčická Brána, the largest natural sandstone arch in Europe.
- Enjoy breathtaking views of canyons, forests, and rock formations.
- **Duration:** Full day.

Dresden Cultural Excursion

- Cross the border to Dresden, Germany.
- Explore Dresden's historic Old Town, including the Frauenkirche and Zwinger Palace.

- Visit museums and galleries along the Elbe River.
- **Duration:** Full day.

Chateau and Castle Tour

- Visit Konopiště Castle, known for its historical significance and beautiful gardens.
- Explore Karlštejn Castle and its medieval architecture.
- Enjoy guided tours of both sites and learn about their history.
- **Duration:** Full day.

Nature and Culture in Brno

- Explore Brno's historical Old Town and landmarks.
- Visit the Cathedral of St. Peter and Paul.
- Enjoy cultural experiences, such as museums and galleries.
- **Duration:** Full day.

MAPS

Prague City Map

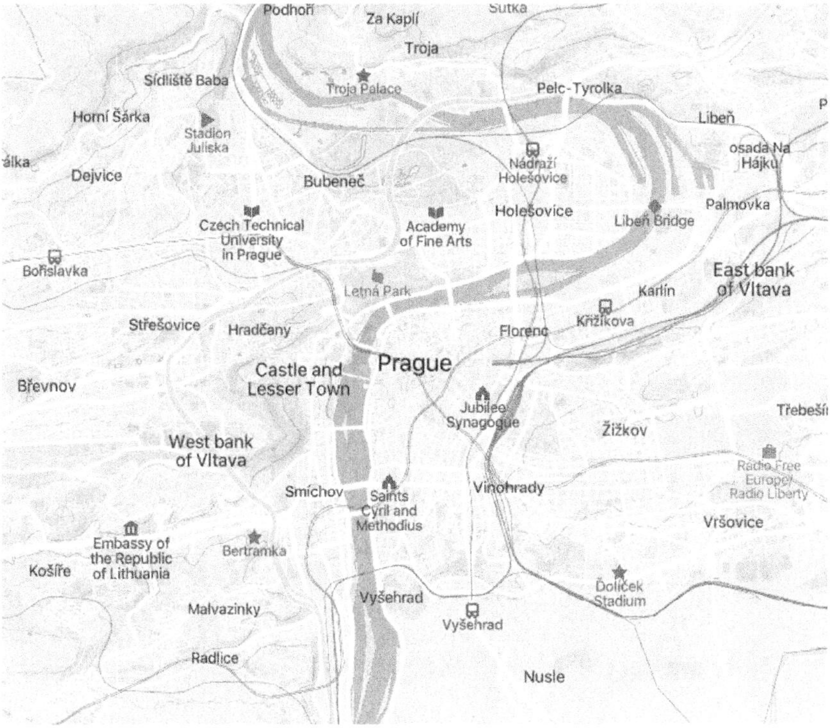

Castle and Lesser Town

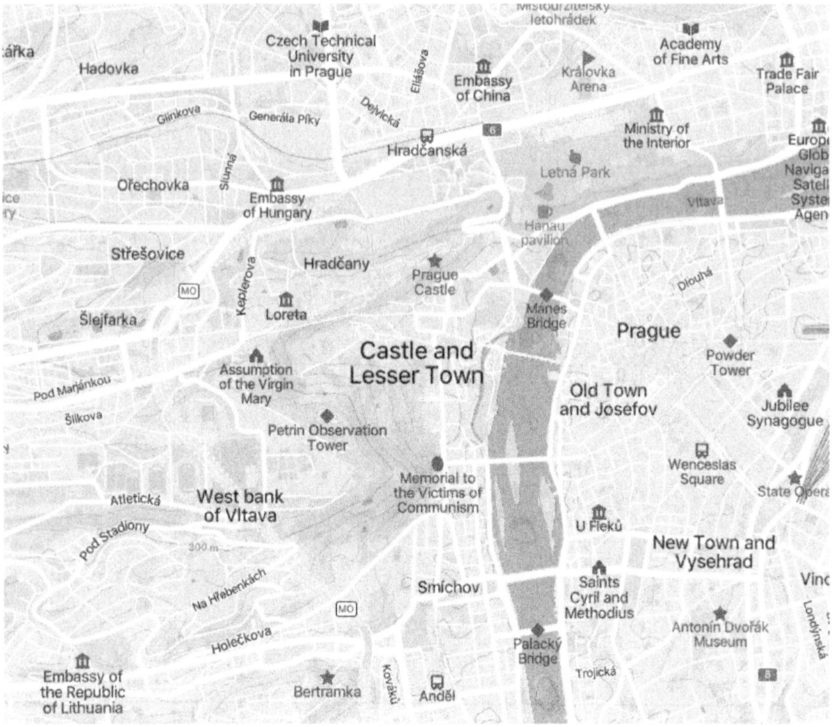

New Town and Vysehrad

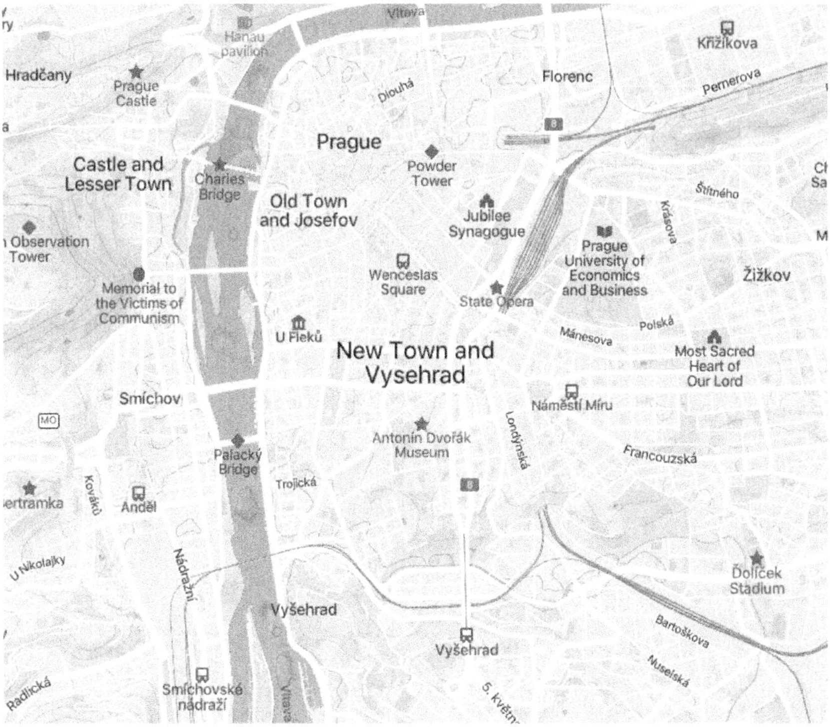

Old Town and Josefov

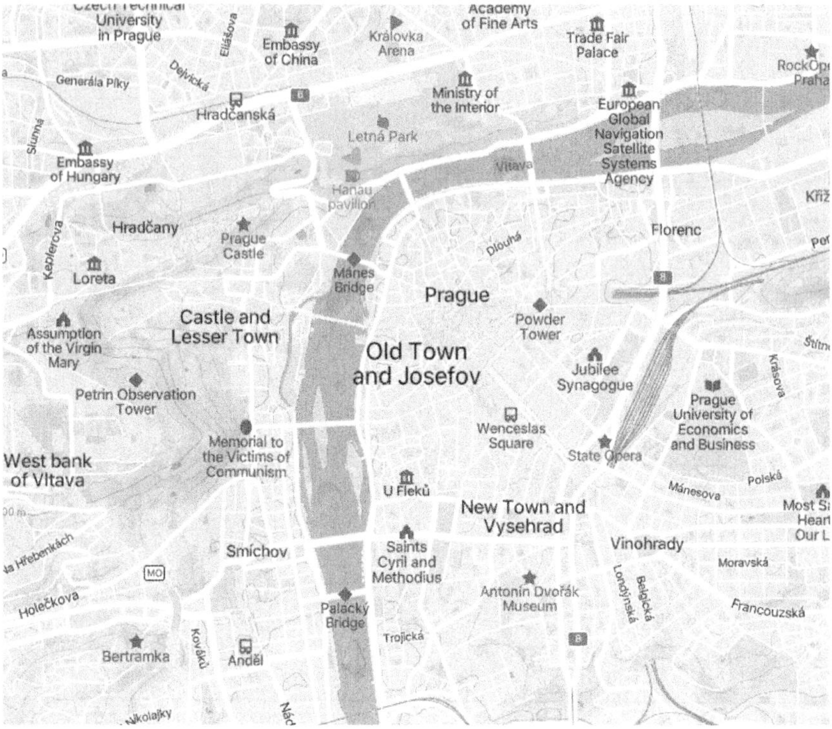

Prague Castle Map

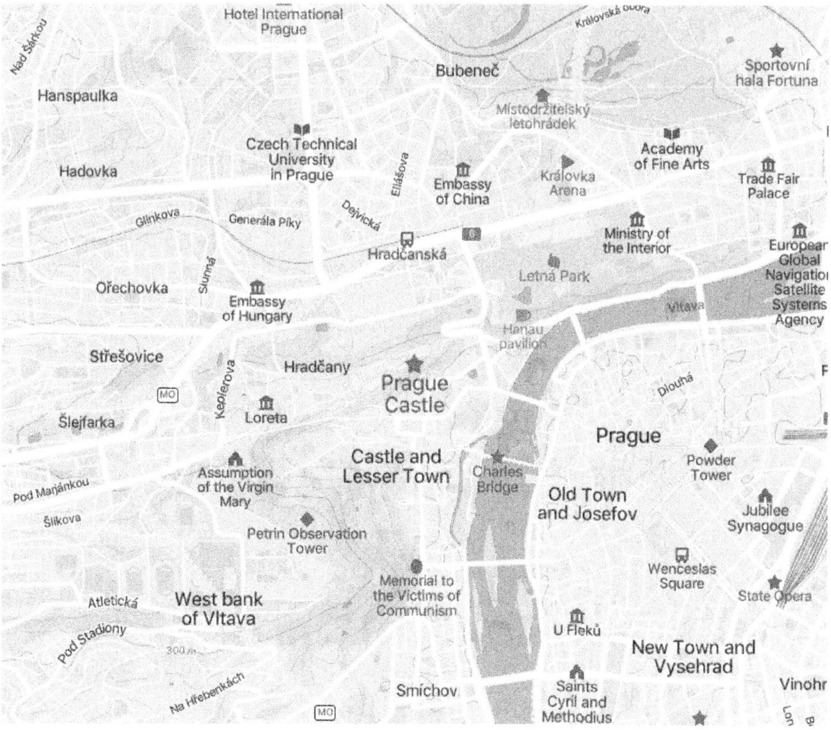

Charles Bridge Map

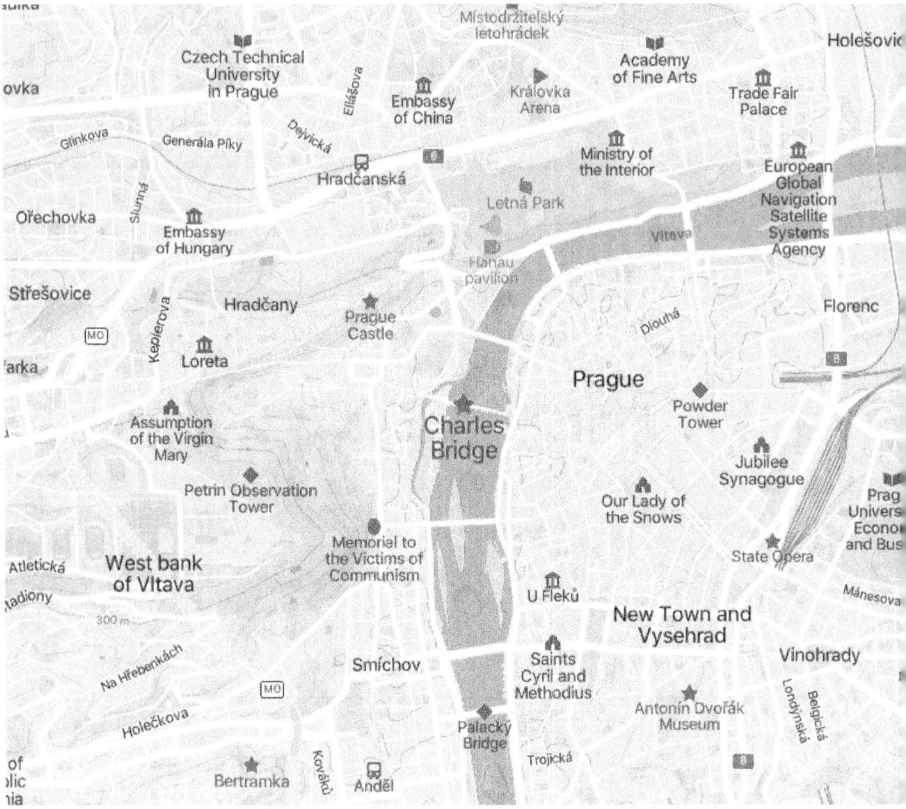

CONCLUSION

As your unforgettable journey through the enchanting heart of Central Europe comes to an end, you will carry with you the memories of Prague's timeless beauty and vibrant spirit. The city's charm, from the Gothic spires to the charming squares, has left an imprint on your soul that will endure for years to come.

Prague's allure is boundless and extends beyond the year 2023. Its rich history and cultural heritage will continue to captivate travelers from around the world for generations to come. As you bid farewell to this magical city, remember that Prague will always welcome you back with open arms, eager to share new adventures and experiences.

May the warmth of the locals' hospitality, the flavors of traditional Czech cuisine, and the echoes of classical music continue to resonate within you long after you depart. Whether you wandered through the historical sites, cruised the river at sunset, or simply soaked in the city's ambiance at a cozy café, Prague has left an everlasting impression on your heart.

So, until we meet again amidst the medieval alleys and under the shadows of the iconic spires, carry the spirit of Prague with you and let it inspire your future travels and adventures. Safe travels, and Na shledanou (goodbye) until your next rendezvous with Prague's enchantment!

INDEX

Printed in Great Britain
by Amazon

33593106R00145